LAMBORGHINI

Other books by this author:

SPORTS RACING CARS
Expert assessment of fifty motor racing greats

SCARLET PASSION
Ferrari's famed sports prototypes and competiton sports cars
1962–73

MASERATI
A racing history

HAYNES CLASSIC MAKES SERIES

LAMBORGHINI

SUPERCARS FROM SANT'AGATA

ANTHONY PRITCHARD

'Tonight at seven o'clock they bring in the Villar bulls. Tomorrow come the Miuras.'

(Ernest Hemingway, *The Sun Also Rises*, Fiesta)

First published in May 2005

A catalogue record for this book is available from the British Library

ISBN 1 84425 094 6

Library of Congress control no: 2005921427

Published by Haynes Publishing, Sparkford, Yeovil, Somerset BA22 7JJ, UK.
Tel: 01963 442030 Fax: 01963 440001
Int.tel: +44 1963 442030 Int.fax: +44 1963 440001
E-mail: sales@haynes.co.uk
Website: www.haynes.co.uk

Haynes North America Inc., 861 Lawrence Drive, Newbury Park, California 91320, USA.

Edited by Jon Pressnell
Designed by Christopher Fayers
Printed and bound in Britain by J. H. Haynes & Co. Ltd., Sparkford

Acknowledgements
I am immensely grateful to those who have helped me and supplied information. Particular thanks go to John Braithwaite, owner of the superb Miura S that is featured both on the cover and within; to Gian Paolo Dallara and Mauro Forghieri; to Cristina Guizzardi at Lamborghini; and to Gary Watkins, who has been a mine of information on the subject of Lamborghini racing. On the practical front, Mike Pullen of Sussex-based Carrera Sport (01444 455100) has been generous in providing guidance on the pitfalls of Lamborghini ownership. Extracts from *Classic & Sports Car* articles are quoted with acknowledgement to the editor, James Elliott.

For help in illustrating the book, warm thanks go to Tim Wright and Kathy Ager at LAT Photographic (Kathy, in particular, has been tireless in tracking down the particular photographs that I have been seeking) and to the staff in 'Stills' at Pinewood Studios, who have done brilliant photographic work for me over the years. Thanks also to Martin Port of *Classic & Sports Car* for his assistance in locating the last key photographs.

Illustrations have been mainly sourced from Automobili Lamborghini Holding SpA and from LAT Photographic (0208 251 3000), photos from the latter coming principally from the archives of *Autocar* and *Classic & Sports Car* magazines. Another valued source has been Bertone, whose press office has, as always, been supremely efficient.

If a source is not acknowledged in the text, then the photo is from the Lamborghini archives.

Anthony Pritchard
Spring 2005

contents

Introduction

Relative to the competition – or at least to the surviving competition – Lamborghini is a youngster. Yet within two years of the sales of its first car, in 1964, the marque had accumulated an enviable prestige, challenging Ferrari and Maserati in the process. Performance, glamour and breath-taking styling were henceforth to be constants for the cars with the fighting-bull badge on their nose.

From the stunning Miura onwards the Lamborghini – almost any Lamborghini – was to be a bedroom-poster symbol of supercardom. But the truth is that despite Ferruccio Lamborghini's ambitions and the vast sums of money poured into the company, it was not commercially successful. Its founder relinquished control in the early 1970s and a roller-coaster succession of owners followed, the company dipping in and out of crisis.

It is only now, under the disciplines of Audi management, that Lamborghini has achieved the goal of efficient production. The marque has become a high-profile division of Audi, still building fantasy cars, but with the major distinction that as well as being superbly engineered they are now exceptionally well developed and beautifully finished.

This book examines the magic of the cars themselves, and chronicles the eventful history of the company

behind them. One of the problems with Lamborghini history, however, is that there are many conflicting statements about the early days of the enterprise. The situation is not helped by the fact that during the period of Indonesian ownership much of the company's archives was destroyed – not even the precise production figures for the Diablo are available. Past written accounts are sometimes very inaccurate, so there is a minefield that I have been forced to wend my way through to the best of my ability. Where I am doubtful of any fact, I have made that clear.

It was with the Miura that Lamborghini took the technical lead. Here, wearing a rather scruffy suit that fell below his usual standards of sartorial elegance, Ferruccio Lamborghini poses with a Miura in 1968. The Miura's transversely-mounted V12 engine at the rear of the car was very advanced for the time. (LAT)

Above: Five decades of mid-engined Lamborghinis, posed outside the company's museum: Miura S to the fore, with a yellow Murciélago behind and at the rear a Diablo 6.0SE to the left and an 'Anniversary' Countach to the right. (LAT)

Left: The Lamborghini badge and Ferruccio Lamborghini's signature as they appear on the original 350GTV prototype.

The Lamborghini *company*

A posed and rather artificial view of a production line in Lamborghini's tractor factory.

Quite why Ferruccio Lamborghini decided to enter the financially risky world of manufacturing high-performance cars has never been satisfactorily explained. It must also be said that there is confused information about both Ferruccio Lamborghini's early days and some aspects of the company's history. All that can be done is to outline his career, give the supposed reasons for his embarking on the venture, set out the views of people who worked with him, and then let the reader form his or her own conclusions.

The son of a farmer, Ferruccio Lamborghini was born on 28 April 1916 in Renazza di Cento, a small agricultural town in Emilia Romagna, the heart of the Po Valley. Conscription into the Italian air force during the Second World War is said to have brought an end to his studies. In the *Reggia Aeronautica* he worked in the section that supplied components and

Ferruccio Lamborghini was a man of drive, energy and vision, who created his own marque – one that despite innumerable problems has survived for more than 40 years.

parts for the repair and maintenance of both trucks and aircraft.

Later he was stationed on the Greek island of Rhodes, where he saw little military action. Following the collapse of the Fascist government, Italy changed sides and joined the Allies, but these events had little impact in the Greek Isles where Lamborghini continued to serve in the air force until the Italian forces on Rhodes surrendered in early 1945. For a short while he was detained as a prisoner of war, but was released and returned home in early 1946.

On his return to Renazza, Lamborghini was struck by the desperate shortage of agricultural machinery, caused to a large extent by Italian industry's concentration on the production of war material. He set up a small engineering workshop, repairing any vehicles that came to hand. Lamborghini married and he and his new wife set off on their honeymoon.

It was while they were away – or so it is said – that he came across some light trucks (some sources say light armoured cars), formerly belonging to the British Eighth Army, that were being sold off at a low price. He bought these and on his return to Renazza he began to build tractors using components from these vehicles.

There was good demand for Lamborghini's creations and his production rose to about one a month. He was also interested in motor sport and he developed and modified 569cc Fiat Topolinos. He claimed to be the first to design an overhead valve conversion for these cars, ahead of Fiat's move to ohv in 1948 for the revised 500B model. In common with other enthusiasts Lamborghini also bored and stroked these engines to a capacity close to 750cc, with the Mille Miglia road race in mind. He drove an uprated and re-bodied Fiat in the 1948 event and, in his own words, 'I finished my Mille

Miglia in an *osteria* [an inn or public house] which I entered by driving through the wall!'

Lamborghini gradually expanded tractor production and began building models of his own design. By 1952 he was designing and building his own engines with two, three and four cylinders, these being modular designs with interchangeable parts. Soon Lamborghini Tractori SpA had moved to new factory premises; by the early 1960s production was running at close to 400 a month, with many of the machines being designed for special applications, and the company was one of the biggest builders of tractors in Italy.

In 1960 Lamborghini diversified into the manufacture of air conditioning and industrial and domestic heating burners, the new company being known as Lamborghini Bruciatori SpA. Both his businesses flourished and Lamborghini became a very wealthy man. He was a highly charismatic,

An early view of the interior of the Lamborghini factory at Sant'Agata Bolognese. Lamborghini understood fully one of the keys to efficient car manufacture: that all the components from suppliers must be boxed or racked for quick location and stocktaking.

engaging figure, exceptionally intelligent yet far from aloof – something that didn't change with his success, which was officially recognised in 1965 when he was honoured with the title *Commendatore*.

There have been quite a number of accounts of why Ferruccio Lamborghini took the decision to enter luxury GT car manufacture. Certainly he had at various times run both Ferrari and Maserati cars, and this can only have influenced him. There are two apocryphal stories in this connection. In both Lamborghini pays a chance visit to Maranello and asks to see Enzo Ferrari. In the one he wishes to discuss the purchase of a new 250GT; in the other he wishes to complain about the clutch on his 250GT. In both versions he is rebuffed. While it would have been be very much in character for Enzo Ferrari to avoid a complaining customer, it does seem improbable that he would have treated a wealthy customer such as Lamborghini in such a fashion.

Ferruccio Lamborghini gave the best explanation himself, reported in a 1964 article by Etienne Cornil in

Sporting Motorist magazine: 'In the past I have bought some of the most expensive gran turismo cars and in each of these magnificent cars I have found some faults. Too hot. Or uncomfortable. Or not sufficiently fast. Or not perfectly finished. Now I want to make a GT car without faults. Not a technical bomb. Very normal. But a perfect car.'

What Lamborghini did not say, of course, was that he also hoped that entering the world of motor manufacture would make him more money. Whatever the mixed motivations, in 1962 Automobili Ferruccio Lamborghini SpA was established.

Work on the prototype Lamborghini was carried out in a corner of the tractor factory while a new factory at Sant'Agata Bolognese – between Modena and Bologna – was being completed. It was, however, first shown to the press in the newly-built car factory, before this was in fact up and running. Sant'Agata is often described as a village, but is in fact a small town, now with some 6,000 inhabitants. Lamborghini built his new factory on a 'greenfield' site, with plenty of room for expansion. The site was chosen for a number of reasons: it was near the existing Lamborghini tractor and oil-burner works but also this part of the Po Valley was depressed and both land and labour

were cheaper than elsewhere. That said, it has been calculated that Lamborghini's own investment from his personal resources and the companies that he controlled equated to £175,000 (approximately $305,000 at today's exchange rates).

In return for agreeing security of employment for the staff, some of whom came from Ferrari and Maserati, Lamborghini was able to augment this with a long-term interest-free loan from the local authority. Those who are familiar with Giovanni Guareschi's Don Camillo stories will not need reminding that this was a strongly Communist region of Italy and that deals with the local mayor were not difficult to strike.

One of Lamborghini's smartest moves was the choice of a fiery, charging bull as the company's badge: Taurus was his birth sign, and he had already used this symbol on his tractors. Other very smart moves were the engagement of Gian Paolo Dallara, ex-Ferrari, ex-Maserati, as chief engineer, and Paolo Stanzani as general manager. Over the next few years the company made good progress, but then in 1971 a combination of problems brought about Ferruccio Lamborghini's downfall, just when he appeared to be on a high.

At Geneva in March that year the company exhibited three production models (Miura, Espada and Jarama) and two prototypes (Urraco and Countach). But the high cost of research and development, coupled with falling production because of industrial problems, high oil prices and economic recession, was bringing the factory to its knees. Compounding this, the introduction of US safety and emission regulations was making it difficult to market cars in America. Nor was the tractor factory in much better financial condition. Already buffeted by recession and by industrial problems, it suffered two other blows: the South African distributor cancelled his entire order, and the new military government in Bolivia, which was a major customer for Lamborghini tractors, dishonoured all the country's financial credit arrangements.

Ferruccio Lamborghini was nothing if not a realist. It was obvious to him that the car company had to go and severe cutbacks had to be made in other areas of his industrial empire. It was much the same decision that Sir David Brown made the same year. He had bought Aston Martin and Lagonda in 1947 and for 25 years car production had been subsidised, one way or another, by the once-mighty David Brown Corporation. To stay solvent he sold Aston Martin Lagonda Limited, and the Vosper shipyard was forced to close, despite a personal injection of £1,000,000 into the company.

By the end of 1971 Lamborghini had succeeded in coming to settlement terms with the automobile company's creditors and this enabled him to keep the company afloat, at least temporarily. Meanwhile he negotiated the sale of a 51 per cent interest in Lamborghini Automobili to a Swiss friend, Georges-Henri Rossetti, whose

family controlled a wide range of business interests including a substantial manufacturer of watch and clock dials. The price is said to have been the equivalent of £300,000.

Lamborghini retained the remaining 49 per cent until 1974 when he sold this to René Leimer, a colleague of Rossetti, whose interests included a cable-laying company; the tractor company, meanwhile, was sold to the industrial group SAME, which went on to become Europe's third largest tractor maker. Lamborghini retained Lamborghini Bruciatori and Lamborghini Oleodynamica, the last of his companies to be formed and a manufacturer of hydraulic valves. His son Tonino became general manager of both concerns.

No longer involved in the day-to-day running of the car factory, Ferruccio Lamborghini retired to his 70-acre estate, La Fiorita, on the shore of Lake Trasimeno in Umbria and there he cultivated his vineyards. In particular he marketed a full-bodied red wine

called *Colli di Trasimeno*, but more usually known as *Sangue di Miura* ('Bull's blood' and not to be confused with the Hungarian wine of the same name). He also produced white wines. Lamborghini did not, however, sever all connections with the car business and was a welcome visitor at the factory from time to time.

During the summer of 1976 Ron Wakefield, European Editor of *Road & Track*, visited the Lamborghini factory, finding it 'depressingly quiet', as he recounted in some detail:

Like the other Italian makers of super sports cars, this small but modern plant in Sant'Agata has taken it below the belt since the energy crisis hit. The assembly lines, which never looked as busy as Detroit's anyway, are well below capacity

Lamborghini loved fast cars, but he also loved the ladies. Here he chats to a young lady at the 1970 Turin show launch of the Urraco. His wife is to his left and her expression seems to say 'here we go again'.

today and one sees just a handful of Urracos here, a few Espadas there and a lot of open space.

There is one bright spot, although on a very small scale: Lamborghini recently increased Countach production and there were six of these ultimate exotica in various stages of completion when I visited the factory, metal craftsmen very carefully working their aluminium panels.

Not all of the activity of Lamborghini is on the assembly lines, however, and one suspects that a lot of the missing people are somewhere else, working on the hotly rumoured BMW project (see page 96), and on a less secretive level the development people are excited about their newest production model, the Silhouette. They're also busy preparing the 3-litre Urraco and Silhouette for American introduction, and if all goes well the two cars will be well along in their EPA certification tests by the time you read this. Wonder of wonders, they are doing the same thing with the Countach and its North American introduction is scheduled for the last

Ferruccio Lamborghini and Gian Paolo Dallara in the yard at Lamborghini. In the background are a row of bodies recently delivered by Bertone.

quarter of 1976. [This was wishful thinking. Neither the Urraco P300 nor the Silhouette made it to the US as official imports, and a factory-sourced 'federal' Countach only arrived in 1986. – AP]

Right now the company is also in the middle of a thorough reorganization and there have been personnel changes since Lamborghini came under Swiss ownership. Commendatore Lamborghini still participates to some extent and I was lucky to see him briefly while there. The new management is gearing up to take on engineering consultancy work in some quantity, which will give Lamborghini something of a Porsche look.

Unlike Porsche, however, Lamborghini intends to do strictly automotive work, while Porsche has done everything from earthmovers to tanks. Concrete details aren't yet available, but the concept seems sound. It seems fairly certain that the Modenese specialists aren't going to recover their pre-crisis levels with superfast cars, and until they can figure out some new magic formula to intrigue the world's moneyed car buyers, it makes great sense to put their tremendous talents and experience on the line for the more interesting projects of more mundane car makers.

The BMW M1 project was, of course, the first of these consultancy projects, but the Lamborghini management was dilatory, development of the M1 for production was very slow, and much of the money went on the development of the Cheetah off-road car. Unfortunately – and as Dallara makes clear – Rossetti and Leimer had no idea how to run an automobile factory. Nor were they prepared to invest the vast sums needed to turn the company round.

Eventually American businessman Zoltan Reti advanced the company a substantial sum of money, but this was secured on the Lamborghini factory, equipment and other assets. Reti realised that he was unlikely to be repaid, so he applied to the court for a winding-up order. In the latter part of 1978 the court appointed a liquidator, Dr Alessandro Artese, and he was given full powers of administration. Artese brought in former Maserati chief engineer Giulio Alfieri to assist, and together they kept the business running, while Artese looked for a buyer.

Ferruccio Lamborghini was approached, but he probably realised that he no longer had the energy and he decided not to become involved again. He had nothing further to do with the company, apart from declining Chrysler's offer of a return to the company in an honorary position in September 1988. He died of a heart attack in February 1993, two months before his 76th birthday. Whatever the outcome, his had been a brave endeavour, tackling the supremacy of Ferrari in the luxury GT market. We will never know just how much Ferruccio Lamborghini was saddened by the necessity of selling the car business. One does suspect, however, that after the first years of car production, without making money, his enthusiasm palled and that he was relieved to be out of such an unpredictable business. It must be remembered that Enzo Ferrari had no real security, and more than enough financial worries, until Fiat acquired a 49 per cent stake in the business and kept it afloat during hard times. At

least Lamborghini was still a very wealthy man when he retired, and he continued to live in comfort and style until his premature death.

In February 1980 the Mimram brothers, 24-year-old Patrick and 35-year-old Jean-Claude, leased the assets of the company. They were enthusiasts for Lamborghini cars, certainly, but they came from a family with extensive business interests and proceeded with caution. Initially they appointed Emile Novaro, a business associate of the Mimram family, as managing director. Both Giulio Alfieri and the sales director from day one, Ubaldo Sgarzi, stayed with the company.

When the time came for the Mimrams to buy Lamborghini outright or pull out of the factory, they bid 3.8 billion lire, the equivalent of £1.25 million, for the assets, and this was accepted. Formal ownership passed to the Mimrams in June 1981. They formed a new company, Nuovo Ferruccio Lamborghini SpA, with the

young but worldly-wise Patrick Mimram as president.

Under its new ownership Lamborghini found some of its former glory. Alfieri introduced the Jalpa, developed from the Silhouette, the engineering team carried out sound engineering development work on the Countach, and the number of employees steadily rose. Lamborghini also pressed on with the development of an all-terrain vehicle – although this proved to be a mistake. Gradually, and crucially, Lamborghini gained a measure of profitability.

By the second half of the 1980s the Mimrams had concluded that the time had come to find a buyer for the company, partly because of the projected high costs of future developments. For some time Lee Iacocca, head of Chrysler, had been making valiant efforts to restore the health of this once-great US company and for some while he achieved good results. He persuaded the Chrysler board that the acquisition of

Ferruccio Lamborghini on the company's stand at Turin for the launch of the Urraco in 1970.

Lamborghini would add to the group's prestige and international standing. The Mimrams agreed an outright purchase by Chrysler at $25.2 million, and the deal was completed in April 1987.

It has been said that to date the Mimrams are the only people to have made money out of Lamborghini. In truth, it is not known whether this is correct, as the Mimrams invested very considerable sums in the company. Whatever the case, at first Chrysler put a great deal of money and effort into Lamborghini, which was reconstituted as Automobili Lamborghini. After 25 years with Ferrari, Mauro Forghieri joined to head a new subsidiary known as Lamborghini Engineering and became Technical Director of the main board. Under Forghieri's overall leadership the company built a V12 Formula 1 engine used by Larrousse,

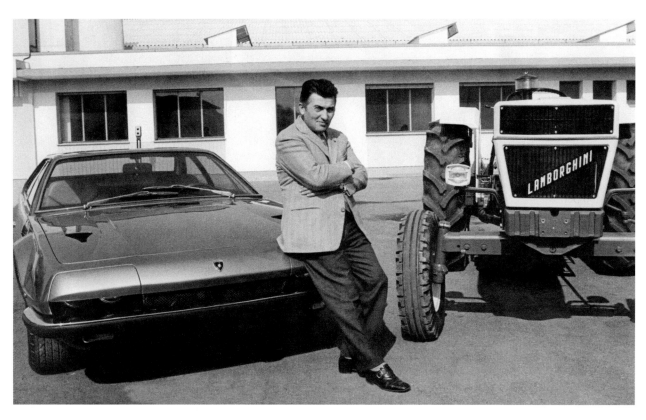

*Lamborghini poses with two of his products: a
Jarama and a tractor.*

Lotus and others, and constructed its
own Formula 1 chassis. Alas, Iacocca's
revival of Chrysler was short-lived, and
car sales plummeted again and there
was no money in the pot to fund
further developments. The greatest
achievement during Chrysler
ownership was the development and
production of the Diablo.

As it fought for survival, Chrysler
lost interest in Lamborghini, and failed
to complete extensive building works
that had been started; it also axed
Formula 1 engine development, in
1993. Meanwhile Lamborghini had
been progressing with the production
of a Gandini-designed smaller-
capacity car coded the P140 and
expected to carry the Bravo name. The
company went as far as entering into a
contract for the manufacture and
supply of the integral aluminium-alloy
body/chassis units.

By some incredible confusion,
Lamborghini executives believed that
Chrysler had given the green light for

production. Whether it had or not
remains a mystery, but as soon as
Detroit realised what had happened,
they negotiated cancellation of the order.
It is understood that Lamborghini had
spent some £13million on the Bravo,
and that this had to be written off. One
of the first reactions was that the sales
director for many years, Ubaldo Sgarzi,
lost complete confidence in the
company's future and took early
retirement in 1992.

It has been calculated that in 1993
Lamborghini lost something over £15
million. Chrysler replaced Emil Novaro
as president with Timothy Adams, a
Chrysler product-marketing executive
whose brief was to find a buyer for the
company. The result was that in
January 1994 Chrysler sold 80 per cent
of its Lamborghini shares to
Megatech, a holding company
based in Bermuda and headed by
Setiawan Djody. The remaining 20 per
cent went to two other companies,
Sedtco and V'Power, but in July 1994
Megatech transferred its shares in
Lamborghini to Sedtco and V'Power. In
all, the sale is said to have realised

$25 million for Chrysler.

Hutomo 'Tommy' Mandala Putra,
son of General Suharto, then ruler of
Indonesia, became president of
Lamborghini, but at the end April 1994
Mike Kimberley, former managing
director of Lotus, took over. His least
popular decision was to impose on the
company a team of British technicians
and management. Later it was learned
that during his regime many of the
company's archives had, for
inexplicable reasons, been destroyed.

The most significant step forward at
this time was the P140 Cala, primarily
a styling exercise commissioned from
Giugiaro's Italdesign. The design
house exhibited the Cala at the 1995
Geneva motor show – at least
demonstrating that Lamborghini's
new owners were making some
progress in the development of a car
to succeed the Jalpa.

But those in Indonesia controlling
the company were losing confidence
in Kimberley, and during 1996 they
appointed veteran Fiat employee
Vittorio di Capua as joint president
with him. As a result of this move,

Kimberley and his British associates left the company. Meanwhile, another major problem was that the Indonesian investors had underestimated the level of capital investment needed by Lamborghini. Cash injections became irregular and there were delays in the payment of suppliers and employees. Di Capua succeeded in bringing the company under financial control by reducing the number of employees by 100 or so, to about 400 people.

Yet another project that failed to enter production was a car powered by the Ford Mustang engine. Designed by Japan's Norbo Nakamura and called the Aerosa, it was intended to have a much lower price than Lamborghinis proper and would have been marketed by Nakamura's company, Gigliato Design. By this time, however, the Volkswagen Audi Group (VAG) had learnt of the possibility of a sale of the company, when Audi was approached by Lamborghini engineers about the feasibility of using an Audi V8 engine and drivetrain in yet another proposed new car.

This led to lengthy negotiations, and in the end VAG brought Lamborghini in August 1998 for an estimated figure of $18 million. Since then the company has operated under the ownership and control of Audi, which has spent vast sums on developing the business, including extending the factory substantially and setting up a fine museum. With serious and well-developed cars, it has succeeded in bringing the battle for supremacy in the supercar market to Ferrari's doorstep. At present the two rivals are both flourishing, but in hard financial times the position could be very different.

Volkswagen now owns three highly prestigious and very expensive marques: Bentley, Bugatti and Lamborghini. It seems inevitable that they will drop one of these famous names, as in truth they have been bought for prestige rather than out of sound economics. Many critics in the industry see Bugatti as a white elephant without a serious future. In contrast, Lamborghini's destiny would appear to be assured,

as under Audi control the company has brought out two well-received and evidently eminently saleable new cars. It seems, therefore, that for many years to come those who are sufficiently well-heeled will be able to indulge in the pleasures of owning and driving a Murciélago, a Gallardo, or one of their eventual successors. Forty-odd years after the company's formation, Lamborghini looks as if it has at last found stability and good health.

Below: In profile the Murciélago is an exceptionally handsome car and one wonders whether future top-of-range Lamborghinis will be able to match its styling. Bottom: At the 2005 Geneva show, Lamborghini exhibited the Concept S, an open car based on the Gallardo and featuring separate compartments for driver and passenger. Despite this anti-social arrangement, the Concept S was greeted with enthusiasm. There were would-be buyers ready to order immediately. Whether a small run would be built, ahead of the planned Gallardo roadster, was not known.

The 350GT
and 400GT

From the rear, the basic lines of Scaglione's body for the 350GTV are similar to those of the production car, but are marked by generous use of chromium plating.

He'd been the wild man of the Bertone design house, and had been responsible for the hallucinatory scroll-winged BAT cars amongst other flights of fancy. So when Franco Scaglione – by then a freelance – was enrolled to style

Ferruccio Lamborghini's new motor car you could be certain the result would cause the odd jaw to drop.

Sure enough, when Lamborghini launched the 350GTV at the 1963 Turin show, it was the star of the event. Sculpted, lithe and lowbonneted, and with a bizarrely deep rear window, Scaglione's flamboyant coupé hid, however, an embarrassing secret: mounted in the display chassis alongside was an impressive all-aluminium V12, but under the sleek bonnet of the car itself was nothing more than a crate of ceramic tiles, to act as ballast.

The reason was simple. Despite its dry sump, the new engine, with its six vertical Weber carbs, was too tall to fit under the bonnet. There was clearly plenty more work to do before the first customer could receive a car bearing the Lamborghini name…

It was also thought – not least, it is said, by Ferruccio Lamborghini himself – that the styling was not quite right; this remains a matter of opinion and some, including Dallara, rate the original style highly.

The model revealed at Turin was known internally as the Tipo 103, having been preceded by stillborn Tipo 101 and Tipo 102 projects, and at its heart was the superb V12 engine designed for Lamborghini by former Ferrari technician Giotto Bizzarrini at his Società Autostar at Livorno.

This uncompromisingly high-tech power unit featured twin overhead camshafts for each bank of cylinders and aluminium-alloy construction throughout, with wet cylinder liners shrunk into the block after machining. It has often been stated that Bizzarrini designed a racing engine, when what Lamborghini wanted was a touring engine, but Dallara has specifically denied this in an interview with the author. The significant point is that Bizzarrini created a remarkably powerful, long-lived and trouble-free design that in developed form still powers today's Murciélago. The Lamborghini V12 engine may not yet have achieved the classic status of the V12 designed by Colombo for Ferrari, but it has the signal virtue of having suffered far fewer launch-time teething problems.

Looking at the engine in more detail, the valves were symmetrically disposed around the cylinder centre-line at an included angle of 70 degrees, with reversed inlet ports and

Lamborghini 350 GT
1964–67

ENGINE:
60-degree V12, front-mounted; aluminium-alloy construction throughout

Capacity	3464cc
Bore x stroke	77mm x 62mm
Valve actuation	Twin overhead camshafts per bank of cylinders, chain-driven
Compression ratio	9.0:1
Carburettors	Six Weber twin-choke 40DCO
Power	280bhp (DIN) at 6500rpm
Torque	239lb ft at 4000rpm

TRANSMISSION:
Rear-wheel drive; five-speed all-synchromesh ZF gearbox; limited slip differential
Final drive 4.09:1

SUSPENSION:
Front: Independent by unequal-length wishbones and coil springs; anti-roll bar
Rear: Independent by unequal-length wishbones and coil springs; anti-roll bar

STEERING:
Worm-and-cam; no power assistance; three turns lock-to-lock

BRAKES:
Front: 11.5-inch (290mm) disc
Rear: 10.8-inch (275mm) disc
Servo assistance

WHEELS/TYRES:
Wire-spoked, centre-lock wheels with triple-eared spinners; 6½in rims
Tyres 205 x 15 Pirelli

BODYWORK:
Two-seat, two-door fixed-head coupé in aluminium-alloy by Superleggera Touring

DIMENSIONS:
Length	15ft 2.6in (4.64m)
Wheelbase	8ft 4.4in (2.55m)
Track, front and rear	4ft 6.3in (1.38m)
Width	5ft 8.1in (1.73m)
Height	4ft 0in (1.22mm)

WEIGHT (KERB):
25.5cwt (1,297kg)

PERFORMANCE:
(Source: *Car and Driver*)
Max speed	156mph
0–60mph	6.4sec
0–100mph	16.3sec

PRICE INCLUDING TAX WHEN NEW:
No UK price quoted
USA (East Coast, Port of Entry): $13,900

NUMBER BUILT:
131

400GT 2+2
1966–68

As 350 GT except:
ENGINE:
Bore x stroke	82mm x 62mm
Capacity	3929cc
Compression ratio	9.5:1
Power	360bhp (DIN) at 6500rpm
Torque	290lb ft at 5000rpm

TRANSMISSION:
Final drive 4.08:1 (3.77:1 and 4.27:1 optional)

STEERING:
Four turns lock-to-lock

WHEELS/TYRES:
Tyres 210 x 15 Pirelli

DIMENSIONS:
Height	4ft 2.6in (1.285m)

WEIGHT (KERB):
28.6cwt (1,451kg)

PERFORMANCE:
(Source: *Road & Track*)
Max speed	156mph
0–60mph	7.5sec
0–100mph	17.8sec

PRICE INCLUDING TAX WHEN NEW:
£6,444 (1967)

NUMBER BUILT:
247

manifolds feeding down between the camshafts. The combustion chambers were semi-hemispherical and the pistons were steeply domed. Inverted bucket-type tappets were used, as on Jaguars, and a duplex roller-chain drove the camshafts. The crankshaft

ran in seven main bearings and each had four retaining bolts, but there were no cross-supports.

In its original form, as installed in the prototype chassis exhibited at the 1963 Turin show, this state-of-the-art power unit had six twin-choke Weber

Right: Ferruccio Lamborghini holds forth on the original prototype 350GTV. Giotto Bizzarrini is second from the right. The dreamer may have departed to pursue other ventures, but relations were good enough for him to be asked to the launch of the prototype. In striped tie is Ferruccio Lamborghini's son, Tonino, and the expression on his face makes it clear what he thought about high-performance cars – not much!

Opposite top: The bug-eyed frontal treatment is one of the weaker aspects of the production 350GT.

Opposite bottom: From this overhead rear view of the 350GT it is easy to see how the enormous rear window gives the interior such a wonderfully spacious and airy feel.

Below: The biggest differences between prototype and production versions are at the front, not least in the prototype's use of concealed headlamps. This historic car is on display in the Lamborghini Museum.

downdraught carburettors and dry-sump lubrication, and developed 350bhp – hence the car being labelled the 350GTV. However, as modified by Dallara for production it had six horizontal twin-choke Webers and wet-sump lubrication. The reason why the inlet arrangement was modified was to ensure that the new car retained as low a bonnet line as reasonably possible.

Transmission was by a five-speed gearbox with synchromesh on all forward ratios, supplied by the German ZF company, and the rear axle incorporated a British-made Salisbury limited-slip differential. As a result of unacceptable transmission noise, after the first 50 cars Lamborghini introduced its own design of final drive, the construction of which was

Above: Stripped of the chromium plating, with half-bumpers and larger rear side windows, the original 350GT is very handsome, with neat, balanced lines.

Right: The 350GT has handsome wire-spoked wheels with triple-eared knock-off hub spinners.

sub-contracted to a local company.

The standard production chassis was of the box-frame type made of rectangular and round tubes, with independent coil-spring suspension front and rear by unequal-length wishbones and combined spring/damper units. Steering was slightly less cutting-edge, in that a worm-and-sector box was used, rather than a rack, but the ZF-sourced box was undoubtedly a good one. Neri and Boancini in Milan built the first 50 chassis and thereafter Marchesi in Modena undertook this work.

The small Sargiotto coachworks in Turin had built the prototype body but did not have the facilities to build series-production bodies and so the company turned to Carrozzeria Touring to hone the styling and body the production cars. By the time that production started, Touring had given the 350GT a conventional if rather

Giotto Bizzarrini: engineer and iconoclast

Although he was a remarkably able engineer, Giotto Bizzarrini was a failure as a businessman. He was neither an 'engine man' nor a 'chassis man', but over the years he dabbled with both disciplines.

Born on 6 June 1926 at Quercianella near Livorno, he graduated in engineering from the University of Pisa in 1953 and lectured there for a short while. In 1954 he joined Alfa Romeo's experimental department, but moved to Ferrari in February 1957. His role at Maranello was as senior engineer and test driver. He was involved in the development of the engine of the Testa Rossa sports-racing car and almost solely responsible for the 250GT swb and 250 GTO competition GT cars.

Bizzarrini was among the 'dissidents' who left Ferrari at the end of 1961. His first independent project after leaving Maranello was the development of the 'Breadvan' version of the 250GT swb for Count Volpi di Misurata, who ran the Scuderia Serenissima Repubblica di Venezia and who had started the ATS company to which most of the dissidents had fled. With a body by Piero Drogo, the 'Breadvan' was a GT car of considerable potential, with a performance comparable to that of the Ferrari 250 GTO, but it was not persevered with – as was, alas, the case with so many of Volpi's projects.

During 1962 Bizzarrini formed his own company, Società Autostar, based at Livorno. He was engaged to help develop the ill-fated mid-engined ATS 2500GT, and was also involved with the ASA 1000GT, a project that had started life as the so-called 'Ferrarina', or small Ferrari. Then came the commission from Lamborghini to design and build a four-overhead-camshaft V12 engine; this was to be the unit that powered the 350GT and its successors. Lamborghini wanted an engine with a net on-the-bench power of 350bhp.

Giotto Bizzarrini, seen at his home with favourite dog and, behind him, a Bizzarrini car – a derivative of the racing Iso Grifo built in the designer's own workshops.

Bizzarrini's engine, designed and built in four months, developed more than 350bhp and it was in effect a full racing engine – at this stage Lamborghini had not made up his mind whether he was going to build a touring car or a racing car.

Once he had completed the engine, Bizzarrini lost interest in it. 'Bizzarrini was always a dreamer', Dallara told the author. 'He was always dreaming of his next project.'

Subsequently, Bizzarrini joined Iso, where he engineered the Rivolta and more particularly the Grifo, both Chevrolet-powered. Renzo Rivolta, controlling director of Iso, died in 1965 and his son Piero assumed control. In 1966 there was an abrupt split between Piero Rivolta and Bizzarrini. Bizzarrini obtained an Order of the Court permitting him to build the racing version of the Grifo

under his own name. In all, 104 of the Bizzarrini GT Strada 5300 (and its GT America derivative) were built, plus six riveted-shell cars harking back to the Iso original.

Bizzarrini also constructed three Strada-based open spiders, a dozen Opel-based GT Europa 1900s, and three mid-engined sports-racers, one of which used a Lamborghini V12. Manufacture at the small Livorno factory ceased in 1968 and Bizzarrini's next project was to undertake the development and construction of the AMX/3 sports car prototypes for American Motors. By then Bizzarrini's financial position was hopeless and he was eventually declared bankrupt. His last venture was a return to then-faltering Iso, for whom he designed the stillborn Varedo prototype exhibited at the 1972 Turin show. From 1972 he occupied the chair in engineering at the University of Pisa and, from 1974, also the same position at the University of Florence.

Above: The cockpit layout of the 350GT is particularly well thought out, with the main instruments either side of the steering wheel, and with a central console of minor instruments, warning lights and switches. It is a far better effort than found on many later Lamborghini models.

Right: The fuel filler is recessed and has a lockable cover.

Far right: An unusual detail is the semi-recessed tail lights with chrome surround.

Opposite: This frontal view emphasises the large windscreen that helps give the cabin such an airy feel, and the single large wiper.

bland appearance, with bug-eyed exposed headlamps and far less ornamentation. Panelling was in aluminium over a tube-steel frame, following Touring's *superleggera* principle. There was good sound insulation and the excellent aerodynamics of Scaglione's original design kept wind buffeting and noise to a minimum.

The 350GT first appeared in this form at the 1964 Geneva show, but production was slow at getting underway, with only 13 cars made that year. Given this hesitant start-up, it is unsurprising that the decision was made to build only the V12 and to abandon for the time being a proposed six-cylinder or eight-cylinder car of about 2.2 litres in capacity. There had also been vague plans to build a competition version of the 350GT with a much lighter, round-section tubular spaceframe chassis

The second 3500GTZ was destroyed in an accident within just a year of being built but the first survives (opposite), and is currently in Arizona. The curvaceous front contrasts with the rear treatment . . . as the shot above clearly shows. The car is built on a wheelbase shortened by 10cm, or roughly 4in. The square-section bumpers are an unusual detail. (LAT)

Left: Neatly styled and beautifully presented, the interior is worthy of a production car rather than a show special. (LAT)

Above: At Turin in 1965 Lamborghini showed this 350GT convertible by Touring. Immediately in front of the camera is the mid-engined Miura in chassis form. (LAT)

Opposite top: The interior of the 350GT convertible: the quality of trim of these early cars is outstanding. On this one-off the centre instrument panel has a softer shape and the switch panel below has a wooden finish not used on regular 350GTs. (LAT)

Opposite bottom: Touring's Flying Star II on the 400GT chassis, exhibited at the 1966 Turin show, looks like a high-speed estate car. It was one of Touring's final efforts before liquidation. (LAT)

and the engine in its original 350bhp form. This, too, was abandoned.

Touring's body was one of Lamborghini's strengths and the quality of construction, the trim and the execution of detail were exceptionally high. Unfortunately, Carrozzeria Touring's insolvency was to prove a major problem. Just as 350GT production was getting into its stride, Touring went into state receivership and deliveries of bodies slowed right off. Following the company's closure in 1967, the last bodies for the 350/400 series were built by Marazzi, an enterprise set up, with ex-Touring employees, by Mario Marazzi, who had

been in charge of Lamborghini body construction at Touring.

On the road the 350GT proved a delight to drive. Apart from the sheer raw power of the V12 engine, it was remarkably flexible and would pull comfortably in fifth gear at 60mph. The handling was superb, partly because of the 50/50 weight distribution front and rear, and the car was completely neutral except under very hard cornering, when a trace of oversteer developed. The unassisted steering was also relatively light, especially taking into account that the 350GT on the road, tanked-up, weighed approaching 27cwt. Braking,

Gian Paolo Dallara – in his own words

I was born in the village of Varano de' Melegari on 16 November 1936 and I studied engineering for two years at Parma University, but they did not have the facilities for me to complete my degree there and so I completed it at the Polytechnic School in Milan.

My wish was to work in the aviation industry and I expected to be offered employment by Aer Macchi. What happened instead was that Ferrari was making enquiries at the university about graduates whom he could employ. I went to work for Ferrari in December 1959 – this, in Italy at least, is the ambition of every young man!

At Maranello I worked in the design department for Carlo Chiti and I was employed in the main on stress engineering. I left in February 1962 and went to work at Maserati with Giulio Alfieri. We were not related, but his father was a friend of my brother-in-law and we both came from Parma. Alfieri had designed the Tipo 60 2-litre and Tipo 61 3-litre front-engined sports-racing cars, which had proved very successful. He had then developed the Tipo 63 rear-engined sports-racing car that had proved a failure. At Modena I worked with him on both the Tipo 64, which was intended as a replacement for the Tipo 63, and on the the front-engined Tipo 151 cars that were raced at Le Mans in 1963 and 1964.

While I was working at Maserati, Ferruccio Lamborghini approached me and asked me to join his new automobile company as chief engineer. He talked to me at the suggestion of Giotto Bizzarrini, who had known me when he was at Ferrari. So I became chief engineer of Lamborghini, but it surprised me then and it still does surprise me that Lamborghini should ask such a young man to be chief engineer – after all, I was under 30 at the time. As assistants, I had Achille Bavini and Achille Pedrazzi, both of whom had

On the right is the young Gian Paolo Dallara at the time he was working for Lamborghini. He still expresses astonishment that Lamborghini should have appointed someone so young as chief engineer. Vic Berris, cutaway artist of Autocar, is in the centre and on the left is 6ft-plus New Zealander Bob Wallace, originally a mechanic but later Lamborghini's development engineer. (LAT)

previously worked for Abarth.

When Lamborghini commissioned Bizzarrini to design the engine, he had not made up his mind whether he was going to build a high-performance road car or a competition car. Indeed, one of the reasons that I had joined Lamborghini was the likelihood that he would enter racing, but he never did so. Bizzarrini

designed a competition engine, so I redeveloped it for touring use and also designed the chassis of the 350GT. We commissioned Scaglione to design the body and I think that he made a very good job of it, possibly better than Touring with the production version.

But Scaglione was a stylist and not a coachbuilder, so we had to find a coachbuilder and we chose Touring. We were not aware of Touring's financial problems; we knew that they had entered into a big contract with the Rootes Group to build Hillman cars under licence, but that was all.

Generally, at this time, what I call 'Modena' cars – Ferraris and Maseratis – lacked adequate heating and air-conditioning, and too little attention was paid to the comfort of the driver; these were the sort of shortcomings that we were trying to eliminate in the 350GT. When the 350GT entered production, it lacked testing. I doubt whether we had done more than 10,000 miles in testing, so the early cars delivered to customers had many faults. There were problems with the ZF gearboxes and so, to some extent, production was limited by the time that we spent resolving problems on early customer cars.

Although Ferruccio Lamborghini did not come to the factory every day, he came at least two or three times a week. We regularly informed him of progress on the Miura and from the start he was enthusiastic about the project. Because of the problems with the ZF gearbox, we designed our own with Porsche synchromesh; it was almost a matter of chance that it had synchromesh on reverse as well as all five forward gears – the position of the gearbox shafts was the reason. There is of course, in the ordinary way, no point in having synchromesh on reverse gear.

After the Miura chassis was so well received at the 1965 Turin show, we looked for a coachbuilder to build the body. We had hoped to use Touring again, but they could no longer undertake the work. So we talked to Bertone, whose first design was absolutely right and needed no changes at all before the car entered production.

In 1968, at the time the Urraco was

being developed, I left to join De Tomaso. There I designed the Formula 1 car entered by Frank Williams and driven by Piers Courage in 1970. I met Piers Courage and Frank Williams at the Mediterranean Grand Prix at Enna in Sicily in late August 1969. Piers won the race with a brilliant, very fast drive with his Williams-entered Brabham and that is how our relationship started.

An agreement was reached that in 1970 Piers would drive the de Tomaso 505 Formula 1 car with Ford-Cosworth engine that I had designed. Piers became a good friend and it was a terrible blow to us all when he was killed in a terrible accident at Zandvoort in the Dutch Grand Prix. Until the end of the year Frank Williams carried on racing the de Tomaso 505 with Tim Schenken at the wheel and then De Tomaso withdrew from racing.

While I was working at De Tomaso, I designed the Pantera, which had a monocoque platform chassis and an American Ford V8 engine. Ford of America was very much involved in

the development of this car, which had a body by Vignale. These cars sold in very large numbers.

I realised that if I wanted to design and build racing cars, I would have to do it on my own, so I set up my own works in my home village and I still have my factory there today. For a brief while after I had started my own company, I worked in 1976 as a consultant for Lamborghini on the later development of the Countach.

Dallara Automobili is a substantial company that builds Indycars and Formula 3 cars. Its cars powered by Chevrolet engines won at Indianapolis in 1998-89 with Eddie Cheever at the wheel and in 2001-02 with Castonaras as driver. The Dallara factory has very sophisticated wind-tunnel facilities, and Dallara also undertakes development work for other manufacturers. The above is based on a 2004 interview.

Gian Paolo Dallara today, behind his desk at Automobili Dallara in Varano de' Melegari, the village in which he was born. (Author)

Top: The quad-cam V12 with its six twin-choke Weber carbs, here the 3.9-litre unit of a 400GT 2+2. Note the alloy castings at the front of the engine, including that for the inverted oil filter. Above: At the front the 400GT 2+2 wears twin headlamps. These rarely enhance a design, but in this instance they add balance to the overall shape. Opposite: From the rear the shallower back window of the 400GT 2+2 is immediately apparent, as is the extra metal between the screen and the rear side windows. (all LAT)

Above: The cockpit of this 400GT 2+2 is virtually unchanged from that of the 350GT, although the seats now have horizontal rather than vertical pleating; a detail difference is that the central panel for the auxiliary instruments has a wood finish. (LAT)

by 11½in Girling discs at the front and 10.8in discs at the rear, was exceptionally firm and positive. Although the roofline was low, the interior in other respects was very roomy and the very considerable area of glass gave the interior a light, airy feel. In contrast, too many, low-slung coupés have depressingly claustrophobic interiors.

All in all, the 350GT was a beautifully balanced and very civilised motor car. Perhaps the highest compliment paid by testers at the time was that they could not make their minds up whether it or the Ferrari 275GTB was the better car. Certainly, general consensus is that the Lamborghini is the quieter.

Of the production run, Zagato

Driving a 400GT 2+2

It's tempting to think that the first model of a new supercar marque created by a tractor manufacturer is going to be at the very least a bit rough around the edges. The surprise – and for the blinkered that surprise will be considerable – is that the 400GT is a fully resolved and crushingly competent car.

The glassy thin-pillared cockpit with its supportive seats and low-key but well-executed trim gets the 400GT off to a good start: later Lamborghinis are less impressive. But the real joy is in the driving, beginning with that sublime power unit. If you're used to the creamy laziness of Jaguar's V12, the Lamborghini is an extraordinary counterpoint. Urgent, hard-edged, with the complementary soundtracks of six Webers, four chain-driven camshafts and two distributors melding in an orchestrated intensity, this is thoroughbred engineering at its finest. But this doesn't translate into fickle undrivability: the torque-rich V12 has a turbine-like power delivery from low revs, easily dosed through a firm long-travel throttle pedal and accompanied by a deep-chested bellowing as you rise through the rev range; yet back off and settle into a motoway cruise, and the engine is contentedly refined.

The Lamborghini-made gearbox is no featherweight, and has a wide gate and strong spring-loading to the third-fourth plane. With a well-weighted and smooth clutch, there's a satisfying beefiness to the drivetrain that is mirrored by the precise and communicative steering. Nothing is too heavy, nothing is too light: the controls are just right for the job in hand.

The chassis has a similar composure. The ride is firm yet sufficiently well controlled to have a degree of suppleness on poor surfaces, all the while with roll held fully in check. The 400GT corners with total composure, taut, balanced, going through the curves with strong reserves of adhesion and a neutral stance. The Lamborghini's underpinnings, in other words, are fully in harmony with the drivetrain.

Those in the know rate the 350GT and 400GT as some of the finest Lamborghinis ever made; that they seem so modern in their comportment on the road is a tribute to the talented engineers behind their creation.

As a driver's car the 400GT 2+2 still stacks up: handling is taut, performance exhilarating. (LAT)

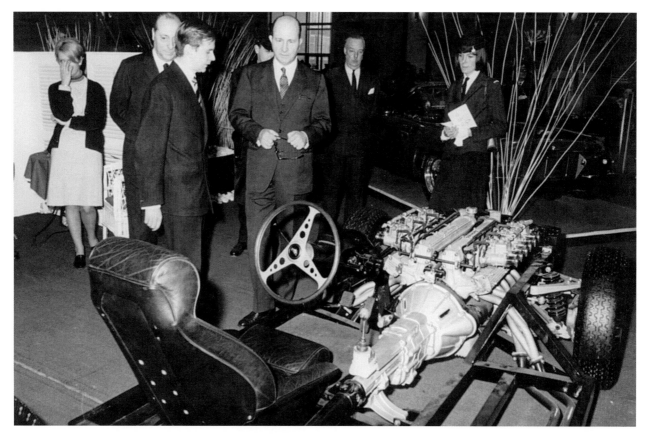

In 1966 Lamborghini exhibited this stripped 400GT chassis at the Brussels show. Obvious features are the square-tube construction and the double-wishbone front suspension.

bodied two cars in very rakish style and these were known as the 3500GTZ. One of these cars was exhibited at the Earls Court show in 1965 and it was rumoured that it was fitted with a 4-litre engine. In addition to the standard production closed coupés, there were also two dropheads built by Touring. Ferruccio Lamborghini admitted that his company lost the equivalent of £400 at 1964 values on each of the early 350GTs he sold, so it is understandable that these never became a production model.

In 1965 the 350GT was offered with a 3,929cc engine, becoming in the process the 400GT; all but three of the 23 such cars built had steel coachwork – a harbinger of things to come. The next stage in the development of this first series of

Lamborghinis came at the 1966 Geneva show, when the 400 GT 2+2 was introduced. Although no longer than the regular GT, the new model had a subtly restyled body with a slightly higher roofline, a smaller rear window, and a larger boot lid; these changes, together with revised rear suspension and a lower rear floorpan, freed up enough room for occasional rear seats to be fitted in place of the luggage platform found on the GT. Twin Hella headlamps each side replaced the single Cibié units, while another detail was that a single fuel tank replaced the twin tanks of the original model. Panelling was now in steel, too, with the exception of the bonnet and the boot-lid.

As far as the mechanicals were concerned, a key difference was the introduction of Lamborghini's own five-speed gearbox with Porsche-licence synchromesh on all gears, including reverse. This took power to a new Lamborghini-made differential, so the drivetrain was now genuinely all-

Lamborghini. The new transmission set-up – and the twin-headlamp front – was phased in on the two-seater models, but few 350 GTs can have been so equipped, as this model was deleted in the course of 1967, after 120 had been made. By this time the 2+2 had become the mainstay model of the series, although the two-seat 400 GT had continued to be offered for a while, after which only the 2+2 was available, pending its replacement in Spring 1968 by the new Islero. In all, 224 of the 2+2s were made, over roughly two years – proof that Lamborghini had truly found its feet as a car manufacturer.

Although the engine was considerably more powerful, it was also torquier, more relaxed and more pleasant to drive – although some minor, irritating faults had not been eliminated. Almost twice as many 400GTs were built compared to the original cars, so a good example is likely to be easier to find.

As Gian Paolo Dallara admits (see

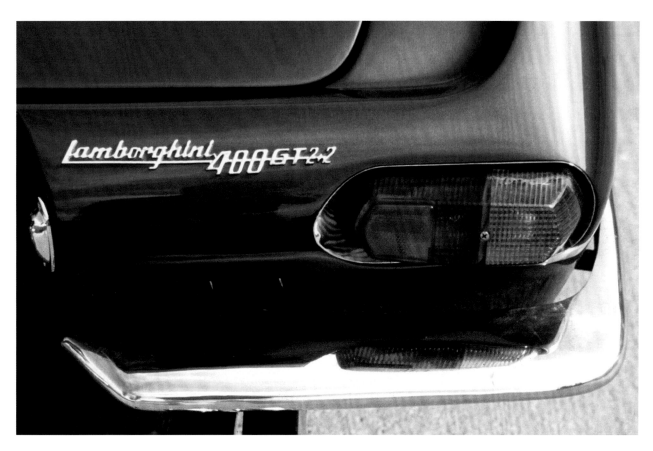

Bold but tasteful badging clearly identifies the 400GT. The details of the body design of these early Lamborghinis are exceptionally neat.

page 29), the 350GT went into production with inadequate testing and development. Many early cars were returned to the factory for modification and these problems interrupted and slowed production in the early months. In any event, it was a bold and wealthy man who was prepared to spend a large sum on a new and untried car, especially if he lived any distance from the factory. For the British enthusiast such concerns were academic, there being no UK importer in these early days. That said, Colonel Ronnie Hoare, of British Ferrari agent and race entrant Maranello Concessionaires, did buy a 350GT direct from the factory. Hoare always had a penchant for unusual road cars and his other purchases included a De Tomaso Vallelunga.

Ferruccio Lamborghini was planning a successor to the 400GT, and Touring

Buying Hints

1. As these are the earliest cars, built only in small numbers, they are the most difficult to locate. They are towards the top end of Lamborghini prices and a purchase should be approached with great caution. A car in poor but restorable condition is unlikely to be economic to tackle. If you find a restored car, then it *may* be a reasonable prospect.

2. Only contemplate purchase if you can examine a full record of the work carried out to the car and can contact the specialists responsible to satisfy yourself as to what was done.

3. The engine is a sturdy unit with a strong bottom end and no obvious weaknesses; parts are available without problem. The transmission is similarly rugged, with slow synchromesh on second the most obvious failing in old age.

4. While mechanical components are relatively easy to source, body parts are almost unobtainable. This need not need to be much of a problem, as specialist panelbeaters can reproduce parts, albeit at considerable cost.

– in its last dying gasp – built a prototype known as 'Flying Star II'. It did not suit Lamborghini's tastes and there were no prospects that Touring

could have put it into production. The solitary prototype was sold and at the time of writing is believed to be in private hands in Britain.

Carrozzeria Touring

This distinguished Italian coachbuilding company was founded by Felice Bianchi Anderloni, born in Rome in 1882 and brought up in Milan. He had family connections with Isotta Fraschini and worked for them from about 1906. He parted company with the Milan company at the end of 1923 and in 1925, together with good friend Gaetano Ponzoni, bought a small company called Carrozzeria Falco that specialised in light framework; Vittorio Ascari (brother of Alfa Romeo racing driver Antonio Ascari) managed the company, but left after about a year.

Anderloni soon changed the name to Carrozzeria Touring – the use of the word 'Touring' has been attributed to a burst of Anglomania in Italy that led manufacturers of basic items, such as soap, to adopt an English-sounding name. It was Alfa Romeo that set Touring on the road to fame and

Purity of line characterises almost all Touring designs. This is a 1940s Alfa Romeo 6C 2500 Sport saloon by the Milan-based company. For many years most of Touring's income came from work for Alfa Romeo. (Alfa Romeo)

Touring in turn did much to enhance the reputation of the Portello factory. Touring established its reputation with Alfa Romeo during the years 1925-27 when it was building coachwork on the Jano-designed 6C 1500 and 6C 1750 chassis. The most dashing were the sports two-seaters or *spiders* and Touring and Zagato vied with each for popularity with Italian sporting aficionados.

Touring bodies were more comfortable and more durable and Anderloni's claims to their lightness angered Ugo Zagato, whose bodies were lighter, but definitely more flimsy. By 1937 Anderloni had perfected his *superleggera* ('extra-light') method of construction, which consisted of a framework of small-diameter steel tubing to which aluminium-alloy sheeting was attached by small wire clips that were bent round the tubing. But although Touring built some exceptionally elegant bodies on Alfa Romeo chassis during the 1930s, the majority of the company's production during this time was rather uninspired coachwork on Bianchi, Fiat and Lancia chassis.

From 1935 Touring had a separate

section for the manufacture of bodies for military and industrial vehicles, and later opened a further section for the fabrication of aircraft components and – in particular – light-alloy welded seat frames. Among Touring's most famous bodies at the end of the 1930s were those constructed on BMW 328 competition chassis. Under Mussolini, there was a reversal of Anglomania in favour of Anglophobia and the company changed its name to *Carrozzeria Turinga*. It reverted to its old name after the collapse of Fascism and added *Superleggera* to the title.

Business was tough in post-war days, so in addition to building bodies for Alfa Romeo, including several thousand 1900 Sprint and Super Sprint bodies, Anderloni took Ferrari on his books and produced the legendary *barchetta* ('little boat') open two-seater body that graced many competition Ferraris from 1948 to 1953. Touring also built prototypes for Aston Martin, Bristol (both of whom adopted its form of construction) and Hudson. Anderloni died on 3 June 1948 and his son, Carlo Felice, who had worked with

him for some while, took control.

Business was slipping away from Touring; Alfa Romeo concentrated increasingly on in-house mass-production bodies and Ferrari took his business to Pinin Farina in 1953 (there were only three more Touring-bodied Ferraris, all built in 1956). In the late 1950s Touring concluded a contract with the Rootes Group to assemble its cars in quantity. Among these was the finned Sunbeam Alpine sports car, from which Touring amputated the fins – this ahead of Rootes so doing. More particularly, it built the Venezia, a Touring-styled coupé with *superleggera* bodywork, based on the Humber Sceptre. To cope with the assembly of the Rootes

models, Touring opened an additional factory and the workforce expanded to about 220. But the licence-built Rootes cars were not a success in Italy and production ceased very quickly. The Venezia was also badly received and only 145 were built between 1963 and 1965.

The Lamborghini contract was too small to save an overstaffed company close to insolvency. The 350 GT was Touring's last production car, and a glorious swansong. It was a triumph of design by a company on its knees. By an order of the Milan court made on 3 March 1964, Touring carried on under administrative control. In early 1966 it was still building some bodies and

One of Touring's most famous designs was the barchetta ('little boat') open two-seater body fitted to competition Ferraris from the Tipo 166 Mille Miglia onwards. Here Dorino Serafini with a barchetta-bodied Tipo 166 is on his way to second place behind team-mate Alberto Ascari in the one-hour production sports car race for cars up to 2 litres at Silverstone in 1950. (TC March/FotoVantage)

one of its final efforts was the Flying Star II on the 400 GT chassis that was revealed that year. Within 18 months of the administration order, Touring was dead; a chemical group took over the factory and burnt the majority of the coachbuilder's drawings and artwork.

The Miura

The Miura chassis at the Turin show in 1965. It is a completely stunning design that combines an audacious concept with surprisingly simple construction. (LAT)

The Miura must be close to heading the list of the greatest supercars of all time. Lithe, sensuous and brutal at the same time, adorned with instantly recognisable trademark details, the Miura's delicious skin is stretched over mechanicals every bit as seductive: a racecar-like steel tub with a mid-mounted V12 set crossways behind the driver's head. Launched at a time when Ferrari was tentatively emerging from years of ironmongerish conservatism, this was the supercar redefined as a heady amalgam of high technology and rolling artwork.

The Miura first appeared, in chassis form, at the Turin show in November 1965. At the Geneva *salon* the following March, the car was seen in prototype form with its glorious Bertone body. This was attributed to Marcello Gandini, then only in his early twenties, who was to become *de facto* chief designer at Bertone following the departure of Giorgetto Giugiario to start Italdesign.

It was at Geneva that the new car first bore the name Miura. It was an inspired name, chosen by Ferrucio Lamborghini, apparently, because his birth sign was Taurus, and it was the name given to a brilliantly fearsome and courageous strain of fighting bull, bred by one Don Miura. Given the factory code Tipo 105, the Miura was to prove the definitive Lamborghini model, the advanced thinking behind its design reflecting the young, ambitious engineering team who wanted to make their mark in the automobile world.

The next public appearance of the Miura was at the Monaco Grand Prix at the end of May 1966, when Lamborghini development engineer Bob Wallace and a mechanic drove the prototype to join the line-up of exotic cars parked outside the casino on the eve of the race. It completely overshadowed the other cars and may have led to a few more orders being placed.

It seems that the engineering staff at Lamborghini, headed by Dallara, had been considering a mid-engined competition car. They discussed the project with Ferruccio Lamborghini and he endorsed instead the development of a mid-engined road car. At this time the use of a mid-mounted transverse engine was almost completely novel and the only powerful cars with mid-mounted engines (longitudinally) were GT prototypes such as the Ford GT40 and the Ferrari 250P and its successors. Once again, Dallara denies specifically that the car that was to become the Miura was designed without Lamborghini's knowledge, as has often been stated.

The chassis was a steel box-section monocoque structure, with deep-section longitudinal members and extensive lightening holes. Two forked radius rods that connected the rear chassis members with the firewall of the passenger area provided additional stiffness; the cockpit area, including the windscreen, contributed to the relief of body stresses and provided additional rigidity to the main structure, although this still – at least initially – left something to be desired. The suspension was the same layout as on the front-engined cars, with thick anti-roll bars front and rear and with the geometry altered to suit the handling characteristics of a mid-engined car. Rack-and-pinion steering, however, was now fitted in place of the previously-used worm-and-sector.

Lamborghini P400 Miura
1966–69

ENGINE:
60-degree V12, mid-mounted transversely; aluminium-alloy construction throughout

Capacity	3929cc
Bore x stroke	82mm x 62mm
Valve actuation	Twin overhead camshafts per bank of cylinders, chain-driven
Compression ratio	9.5:1
Carburettors	Four Weber triple-choke 46IDA 3C1
Power	350bhp (DIN) at 7000rpm

TRANSMISSION:
Rear-wheel drive; five-speed Lamborghini-made gearbox with synchromesh on all ratios including reverse; ZF limited-slip differential Final drive 4.052:1 (4.33:1 and 4.05:1 optional)

SUSPENSION:
Front: Independent by unequal-length double wishbones and coil springs; telescopic dampers; anti-roll bar
Rear: Independent by unequal-length double wishbones and coil springs; telescopic dampers; anti-roll bar

STEERING:
Rack-and-pinion; no power assistance; 3.2 turns lock-to-lock

BRAKES:
Front: 11.8-inch (300mm) Girling disc
Rear: 12.1-inch (307mm) Girling disc
Servo assistance

WHEELS/TYRES:
Cast magnesium-alloy wheels with triple-eared spinners
Tyres 210 x 15 Pirelli Cinturato HS

BODYWORK:
Two-seater fixed head coupé in aluminium-alloy by Bertone

DIMENSIONS:
Length	14ft 3.5in (4.36m)
Wheelbase	8ft 2.6in (2.50m)
Track	4ft 7.5in (1.41m)
Height	3ft 5.5in (1.06m)

WEIGHT (KERB):
18.6cwt (943kg)

PERFORMANCE:
(Source: *Sporting Motorist*)
Max speed	170mph
0–60mph	4.9sec
0–100mph	11.7sec

NUMBER MADE:
474

P400S Miura
1969–71

As P400 except:
ENGINE:
Compression ratio	10.7:1
Carburettors	Four Weber triple-choke 40IDL 3L
Power	370bhp (DIN) at 7700rpm
Torque	286 lb ft at 5500rpm

TRANSMISSION:
Final drive 4.08:1

WEIGHT (KERB):
25.6cwt (1,298kg)

PERFORMANCE:
(Source: *Autocar*)
Max speed	172mph
0–60mph	6sec
0–100mph	15sec
50–70mph in top	9.5sec

PRICE INCLUDING TAX WHEN NEW:
£10,860 (1970)

NUMBER BUILT:
140

P400SV Miura
1971–72

As P400S except:
ENGINE:
Power	385bhp

WHEELS/TYRES:
15in wheels with 7in front rims and 9in rear rims

DIMENSIONS:
Track, front	4ft 8in (1.412m)
Track, rear	5ft 0.6in (1.541m)

PERFORMANCE:
Max speed	180mph

NUMBER BUILT:
150

Above: Here the tub is panelled-up and ready to be mechanised.

Right: The basic monocoque 'punt' of the Miura is an impressive piece of fabrication, liberally punched with lightening holes.

As installed in the Miura the 4-litre engine had downdraught carburettors: there were not the same critical height considerations with a rear engine, and the mounting of the carburettors in the vee of the engine permitted much simpler inlet tracts. In its original form the Miura had a power output of 350bhp at 7,000rpm.

The casing of the five-speed gearbox was cast in unit with the engine and final drive, and the power between the clutch mounted on the end of the crankshaft and the driveshaft was transmitted by an idler shaft, in the same way as on a Mini. Also as on a Mini, the engine, gearbox and differential shared the same oil supply. Some owners regard this as unsatisfactory and have had their cars modified so that the oil supply is split.

Left: At the 1966 Geneva show the prototype Miura appeared in startlingly handsome completed form, with its Bertone body – and at last the penny dropped that it was intended for production. Here the Miura is being unveiled to the press on the Bertone stand. Look behind and you'll see a forgotten Bertone one-off, a 911-based Porsche roadster.

Below left: A production Miura: the Miura was the most exciting supercar of its era, with a very advanced specification and an outstanding performance.

On the first three Miuras the crankshaft turned anti-clockwise and there was a Borg & Beck triple-plate clutch. Thereafter Dallara reversed the crankshaft's direction of rotation, having found that the engine ran more quietly in this form. He also substituted a single-plate clutch that transmitted the power through helically-cut spur gears. Lamborghini tried both hydraulic and cable-operated gearchanges, but on the production cars a mechanical linkage was used, running more directly through the floor tunnel and the crankshaft housing. This goes a long way towards explaining why the gearchange is so heavy.

Lamborghini used massively powerful twin-circuit Girling disc brakes front and rear, and there were

Who styled the Miura?

The Miura is generally credited to Marcello Gandini, who joined Bertone as *de facto* chief stylist in November 1965, following the departure of Giugiaro to set up his own studio. It seems, however, that the origins of the car's lines are less straightforward. In an interview with Giugiaro in 1995, for *Classic & Sports Car* magazine, journalist Peter Robinson was shown a sheaf of sketches dated October and November 1964 that clearly prefigure the design of the Miura. 'When I left Bertone I didn't have a chance to follow the building of the car, but the originals of these drawings stayed behind,' Giugiaro told Robinson. 'Gandini took my sketches and finished the car – 70 per cent of the design is mine.'

This is intriguing stuff – and not the first time that the paternity of a design has appeared ambiguous. House style tends to evolve in a coherent manner, though, whoever is at the helm, so at the very least one would expect some continuity as the direction of Bertone's styling moved from Giugiaro to Gandini.

It is worth signalling, in this context, that the treatment of the side windows of Giugiaro's 1963 Testudo, and its lie-flat headlamps, can be seen in the Miura, while the sensuous sweeping flanks of his 1964 Alfa Romeo Canguro also find an echo in the Lamborghini.

15-inch magnesium-alloy wheels cast with spokes so shaped as to aid brake cooling. As for the body, the failure of Touring meant that Lamborghini had to come to terms with another coachbuilder; accordingly he commissioned Bertone to do the job. The result was magnificent: a coupé

Lamborghini exhibited this Miura roadster at the 1968 Brussels show, but it did not progress beyond the prototype stage. Subsequently a couple of owners have had their Miuras rebuilt in this form – arguably a misguided way to ruin a classic design.

with superbly balanced lines that combined the bravura of a competition car with a reasonably good level of finish. Not only that, but the Miura was also surprisingly compact for its configuration.

The one-piece aluminium-alloy nose and tail panels rose to give good access to the engine and luggage accommodation at the rear, and to the spare wheel, radiator and fuel tank at the front. The passenger compartment was insulated from the engine compartment by a single glass panel and the small luggage area was in the tail behind the engine. The simplicity of line was marred slightly by the heavy slatting over the shallow slope of the rear window (rearward vision through the interior mirror was almost non-existent) and by the fussy 'eyelashes' above and below the headlamps. The slatting did however serve to extract engine heat into the atmosphere and away from the occupants.

On the prototype the 'eyelashes' tipped forward with the headlamps and looked plain silly. In any event, they were a styling feature that the

This angle shows off the superbly well-balanced lines of the Bertone-bodied Miura S. The car is owned by John Braithwaite. (FotoVantage)

Far left: Headlamp detail of the Miura S: the headlamps pop up, but the 'eyelashes' are fixed, although the top ones rose up with the headlamps on the prototype Miura. (FotoVantage)

Left: Hidden behind the grille on the left side of the bonnet is the filler for the radiator. (FotoVantage)

On the road with the Miura P400S

Although the Miura is only 3ft 6in high, the big, wide-opening doors make it an easy car to get in and out of; the driving position, though, is laid back, and it takes drivers accustomed to more upright vehicles a little while to adapt. To start the V12 engine from cold, the driver prods the accelerator pedal to the floor two or three times and then it fires up readily, settling into a deep rumble on tick-over.

Once the car is on the move, the engine note turns into a raucous bark that is almost socially unacceptable even at low engine speeds and this alone is enough to make the Miura unsuitable for everyday use. The acceleration is fierce, incredibly fierce, but relentlessly smooth, accompanied by the crescendo of the exhaust.

The Miura has the gearlever moving in an open gate, and it is a heavy but positive change with a long movement. Consequently if the driver is trying hard, the slow change means that the revs drop off too much between gears. Likewise, as was so typical of Lamborghinis for many years, the steering, although extremely positive and taut, is rather on the heavy side and it is hard work to manoeuvre the Miura at low speed.

An interesting aspect of the Miura and all subsequent Lamborghini cars is the gearbox with synchromesh on reverse. It does enable reverse to be engaged silently and, but for the safety catch, there would be a very real risk of engaging reverse when travelling forwards – with potentially disastrous results. If you have driven, for example, an early Porsche 911, with the same gear pattern – of first down on the left, reverse ahead of it, and then across the gate for the four upper gears – then you may have memories of clonking against reverse to the accompaniment of unpleasant grinding noises, as you change up through the box. Porsche gearboxes seem to take this mistreatment in their stride, but with Lamborghinis the safety catch is a vital device to prevent disaster.

On the open road the Miura rockets effortlessly past slow traffic. The acceleration is matched by superbly powerful brakes, recalling the old truth that speed is safe if used sensibly. With a front-to-rear weight distribution of about 45:55 (with a half-full tank), and with such positive steering and well-sorted suspension, the handling of the Miura is generally neutral, but extremely hard driving can provoke a small degree of oversteer. Adhesion is exceptionally high, there is no noticeable roll, and you are firmly gripped in the very comfortable bucket seats. Over bumpy roads, the Miura bounces around a little, but no more so than many modern high-performance cars.

You cannot escape the exhaust note of the Miura and this is accompanied by the mechanical noise that you would expect from a high-performance engine with four chain-driven overhead camshafts. It means that driving the Miura is exhilarating and above all tremendous fun. Noise apart, there are no problems if you want to go touring in the Miura, except that as your luggage is in such close contact with the engine, it does get rather warm. The fuel capacity is 17 gallons (77 litres), and at 14mpg this gives an adequate range of 230–240 miles.

The rear window slats are the least satisfactory aspect of Miura styling, but are a distinctive feature of the model. (FotoVantage)

Miura could arguably have done without. The headlamp mechanism was actuated by a switch near the gearlever, while the switch for the lights themselves was one of a bank mounted in the roof panel.

For many years Lamborghini struggled to achieve a satisfactory instrument layout and this was one of the poorer features of the Miura. There was a large speedometer and tachometer in front of the driver, but the rest of the instruments were out of the driver's natural sight line, grouped in a central cowl. Although the Miura's trim seemed to be made to a high standard, with neatly-stitched padding and upholstery, the quality was not high – until the SV the seats weren't even leather – and trim durability was poor. It was not unusual for owners to have their cars re-trimmed immediately after they had taken delivery – although not necessarily in the wild-boar hide specified by Frank Sinatra for his Miura. Another unfortunate fault of Miuras was a tendency to catch fire when the carburettors flooded and quite a number of cars are rebuilt survivors of self-conflagration.

Production did not start until late 1966 and demand exceeded even the most optimistic expectations – originally, the company thought that it would be lucky to sell 50 Miuras. The early cars were still being developed during production and many enthusiasts prefer the later versions, which tend to be more reliable.

When the Miura was introduced, there was no direct rival and it took some while for the opposition, especially Ferrari, to catch up. De Tomaso built the Mangusta with a Ford V8 engine mounted longitudinally at the rear and although it was a very underrated car, much criticised by those who had never driven one, it was not in the same league. Ferrari did not at this time offer a mid-engined car – although the Dino was soon to emerge – and Maranello had no serious rival to the Miura until the company introduced the Berlinetta Boxer with its flat-twelve 4,390cc engine in 1973 – by which time, of

course, Lamborghini had further moved the game on with the Countach. As for Maserati, its V8 4,719cc mid-engined Bora only appeared in 1971.

The Miura entered production at a time when Lamborghini was expanding the factory and taking on more staff. Yet despite this, the whole team at Sant'Agata had very conservative views on the Miura's sale potential. There was the belief that its specification was too advanced for most buyers and it was doubted whether as many as a revised estimate of 100 could be sold. Ultimately this

The 4-litre V12 engine is mounted transversely at the rear; thanks to the one-piece tail that can be lifted to a vertical position, accessibility is excellent. (FotoVantage)

figure was vastly exceeded.

As with all very fast cars, there was a lot of talk of very high maximum speeds. Some suggested a figure of 180mph, while the factory reckoned 170mph and *Road & Track*, the influential American magazine, achieved 168mph at 7,375rpm with the later 400S. Although the later cars referred to below were more powerful, there was no improvement in maximum speed. It was all pretty academic anyway, as no owner in his right mind would try to emulate road test maxima achieved under very

special conditions – a long, clear stretch of road without the likelihood of any other traffic appearing, a good smooth surface with plenty of grip, and minimal or nil wind. What the lucky owner was likely to do at best was to cruise at around 130-135mph and that required considerable concentration on an ordinary motorway, even under very quiet conditions.

The journalists of *Road & Track* summed up the Miura neatly: 'We've never kidded ourselves that the Miura is a practical automobile; instead it

should be considered an exercise in automotive art – a design for a particular type of driving that can be practised only rarely. Its price assures that it will be owned only by people who can afford other cars for other purposes and, taken in this context, it is a masterpiece to be relished by the connoisseur.' Fairer than that you cannot say.

In 1968 the company introduced the improved P400S, which had a slightly greater power output of 370bhp, mainly as the result of new camshafts, and also had a stiffened chassis,

Racing the Miura

Dallara always wanted to build racing cars and there is little doubt that he hoped Lamborghini would authorise a racing programme. It was not to be: generally the Miura was not regarded as suitable for racing. Despite this, the cars have made a few race appearances. The Steinwinter Racing Team in Germany, for instance, ran a car in a few events in 1968 with Gerhard Mitter at the wheel, but it was not

conspicuously successful.

On the other side of the Atlantic, meanwhile, a Miura engine race-developed by Bob Wallace was supplied for competition work to a buyer in Salt Lake City, Utah. In England, Mark Walker campaigned a Miura in British club racing in the 1980s, but it was less than reliable because of oil-pressure problems.

This reflects one of the main reasons why Miuras have not been

Ferruccio Lamborghini disapproved of racing, but some private owners competed with their cars. This is the Steinwinter Racing Team car at the Nürburgring with Gerhard Mitter at the wheel. (Author's collection)

raced more often: when the car is cornered very hard, there is considerable oil surge and the baffles in the sump of the transversely-mounted engine do not control this adequately.

Above: A superb shot
of the frontal aspect
of the Miura 400SV
– an awe-inspiring
sight in the rear view
mirror.

Left: A view of the
400SV with front
and rear covers open.
It is a handsome
beast by any
standard.

Bob Wallace and the Miura

In 1963 New Zealander Bob Wallace, accompanied by Chris Amon, called at the Lamborghini factory, looking for a job. He joined the company as a mechanic, but soon showed that he had excellent driving ability and possessed that rare quality of being able to explain clearly what the problems were with the cars. He was promoted to development engineer and conducted most of the test-driving of prototype and pre-production Lamborghinis during the years he was at the factory.

The motoring press respected his driving abilities and he enjoyed an exceptional relationship with most leading motoring journalists. Not only did they trust his driving, but they trusted him as a man. Furthermore, as an English-speaker he was able to deal with American customers so much more comfortably than any Italian could.

In an article published in *Road & Track* in 1998, Wallace recounted some of his memories of the Miura. 'When the Miura became an overnight success, we needed the money so we rushed ahead with production, building more cars than we'd ever

planned, before the development was completed. For that reason, the later S and SV were better sorted', he recalled.

'With the Miura, you could go to Rome in two hours twenty minutes. Then you make the run from Rome to Naples (142miles) in less than an hour. The competition tested its cars the same way. All the factory drivers would clock in on the autostrada toll and get a Milan-to-Modena time. Everyone would try to beat the record. My fastest time was 38 or 39 minutes for the 106-mile distance, averaging well over 160mph.

'I'd go hunting for a Daytona or a Ghibli with *Prova* plates and we'd run each other down the road. While we never compared notes on the cars, we

Driving a Miura 400SV the way that a Miura should be driven. They handle beautifully in the right hands.

did become fairly good friends with the Ferrari and Maserati testers.'

Bob Wallace left Lamborghini in 1975, at much the same time as Paolo Stanzani. His reason for leaving was that Lamborghini had no new projects for development testing and he could see no future for himself at the company. He went to the United States and joined the Harrah Automobile Collection where he worked on car restoration. Later he set up a car restoration business, specialising in Ferrari and Lamborghini, based in Phoenix, Arizona.

revised rear suspension, and constant-velocity driveshafts; the brakes on later versions of the 'S' were better, too, thanks to the phasing-in of ventilated discs. Air-conditioning and electric windows were now optional, also, according to the market in which the cars were being sold.

A one-off variant of the Miura, the P400 roadster, was exhibited at the Brussels motor show in 1968. Gandini had carried out detailed restyling, mainly aimed at improving airflow and reducing buffeting. Although the roadster attracted substantial interest, Ferruccio Lamborghini refused to

sanction production, mainly because he did not consider that the company could sell enough cars to satisfy the minimum order of 50 bodies required by Bertone.

Lamborghini sold this car to the American-based International Lead Zinc Research Organization who had

the car dismantled and reassembled after components had been plated with their products. It was used for promotional purposes, before being exhibited in a museum; eventually it was sold to Japan. Since then, private owners have converted Miuras into roadsters, but in the author's opinion

this seems merely an effective way of ruining a classic car.

At the 1971 Geneva motor show Lamborghini introduced the ultimate Miura, with stronger performance and much improved handling. Called the 400SV, it had a 385bhp engine, with separate lubrication for the engine

A magnificent view of the 400SV double-wishbone rear suspension clearly showing the coil-over-damper units and the anti-roll bar with its long actuating arms, as well as the drilled channel-section rear of the chassis.

Miura SV – a dream come true

Mark Hughes was fortunate enough to be able to drive – on Italian roads – probably the best Miura SV in the world. The experience was a memorable one, as he related in the pages of Classic & Sports Car *magazine:*

It's a moment of revelation. After wondering for most of my life what it must be like to drive a Lamborghini Miura, the car I consider the most beautiful ever made, its awe-inspiring abilities sharpen into perfect focus. With the Miura, especially in definitive SV guise, looks don't deceive...

The sun is shining, the scenery is breathtaking and the road is challenging. I'm beginning to feel at ease with the car, ready to push it a little harder. Braking firmly into the hairpin, down into second gear, caressing the steering into the turn, squeezing on the throttle again, bracing my body as the rear wheels chew into the road, building the revs as the road straightens, cacophonous howl from the engine, intense thrust before easing the gearlever into third, surging through the next curve as if it isn't there, right foot still on the floor, tug the shift back for fourth...

The Miura is suddenly all that I had imagined it to be. My soul is not merely stirred – it's shaken.

Ahead, beyond those voluptuous front wings, the road is one of Italy's best, corkscrewing for 15 miles along the hilly coast between Rimini and Pesaro...

How exquisite [the] handling is. If you were to single out one mechanical element as an example of how the Miura does things, it has to be the steering. The leather-bound rim of the three-spoke wheel is slender and invites you to hold it gently, which is the right way to take the reins of a Miura. Light in feel, fluid in movement and uncannily communicative, the unassisted rack-and-pinion system gives millimetre-perfect control and an extraordinary sense of oneness with the car. There's none of the self-centring of modern cars, but having to unwind lock adds to the sense of complete command. There's genuine

tactile pleasure, too, in guiding a Miura, whether round street corners or through fast bends.

Motoring hard, but still directing the car with fingertips and palms, you feel every subtlety of road surface, tyre loading and stance. No other car gives such detailed, precisely tuned messages from the world outside, an attribute that makes the Miura intensely involving to drive, yet at the same time surprisingly easy to propel quickly. Some high-performance cars are intimidating, but the Miura feels familiar and trustworthy.

How a Miura handles in real anger on the track I can only speculate, but in brisk open-road motoring it has such reserves that there's little to say except that it goes where it's pointed . . .There's a mild feeling of the front tyres (215/65) trying to run wide under hard acceleration, but never a hint that the rears (235/60) want to break free. Stability at speed is exemplary.

Allied to the Miura's purity as a sports car, though, is a welcome degree of ride comfort. The suspension is stiff and the body doesn't roll, but there's just enough compliance to remove any harshness when the going gets rough. For a machine of such awesome performance, the Miura's refinement is such that you can genuinely imagine living with one daily.

That is if you don't mind some engine noise. When you see one cylinder bank of the V12 and a pair of gigantic Weber carburettors through the perspex panel behind the seats, you expect that progress in a Miura won't be peaceful. It isn't. Four triple-choke carburettors, 12 pistons, four camshafts, 24 valves and one timing chain create a gnashing frenzy inches from your ears – and that's only at tickover. The sound echoing around the cockpit swells to something more melodious when you're motoring, and all the time it's overlaid by the gutteral bellow exploding from twin tailpipes.

Beyond its aural delights, the V12 delivers the performance you expect from 385bhp in a car weighing only 1200kg. The Miura squats slightly

when you unleash the power, surging forward with relentless force until you pause – at 8,000rpm if you dare, but 6,500rpm seems prudent in somebody else's car – for the next gearchange.

Apart from sheer muscle, flexibility is this engine's strong feature. It tolerates 1,500rpm reasonably happily in any gear, although there are a few induction splutters until you pass 2,500rpm. From there it pulls strongly and seamlessly, delivering a distinctly more intense shove approaching 4,000rpm, and a broad sweep of vivid acceleration thereafter . . .

My guess is that an SV will hit 60mph in just under 6 secs, a time that would be significantly better but for the Miura's single flaw. The sluggish gearbox . . . means that acceleration is a series of sharp bursts with long pauses in between.

Despite looking the part with a typical Modenese metal gate at the root of a stubby lever, the gearchange is heavy, sticky in movement and occasionally baulks. You get used to it, but there's an imbalance between the relaxed fingers of one hand gently guiding the steering and the muscles in your other arm tensing to move the gearlever.

The floor-hinged foot pedals are also on the heavy side, but feel right. The big throttle has a stiff but smooth movement, the brake pedal needs a good push to bring life to the all-round discs, and the clutch, while weighty, allows such a progressive engagement that you can pull away from rest without twitching the revs above idle . . .

The glassy cabin is wonderful. Trimmed in white and black leather, it's roomy for two, feeling broad and surprisingly tall given the car's low-slung build. All the same, you feel as if you're lounging on the road . . .

Few cars in my experience have exceeded expectations but the Miura, with its blend of sensational dynamic abilities and a sufficiently peacable disposition, undeniably did. And that's the view of someone who placed the Miura on a pedestal 25 years ago . . .

Above: The transversely-mounted V12 engine of the 400SV Miura with four triple-choke Weber carburettors.

Left: The interior trim of the Miura 400SV is of much better quality and far neater than that of the earlier examples of the model.

Jota – a very special Miura

The Jota is a version of the Miura developed by Bob Wallace and built in 1971. The lines are generally sleeker, the air intake is shallower and the headlamps have been recessed behind plastic cowls.

This car, properly called the Miura S Jota, was a project undertaken in 1970 by Bob Wallace, to create a Miura S suitable for GT racing. Wallace substantially altered the suspension geometry, modified the engine, reduced weight, fitted larger rear tyres, and improved straight-line adhesion by adding a neat front spoiler. The Jota was also the first Miura to have separate lubrication systems for the engine and transmission. As for the name Jota, this derives from a type of Aragonese dance, usually performed by the public in the street during the fiesta held at a corrida.

Wallace was very pleased with the car and hoped that he would be allowed to race it, but Ferruccio Lamborghini was not interested in racing, being well aware that so many racing projects failed and did the car's maker nothing but harm. Not unexpectedly, then, Lamborghini would not permit the car to be raced

and it was sold to an Italian enthusiast. Unfortunately the new owner's mechanic took the car out and hit a bridge, the resultant fire destroying the car.

There have been replicas based on production Miuras, and racing driver Hubert Hahne, the Lamborghini agent in Germany, is said to have built eight such cars; in all cases they cannot be regarded as satisfactory in terms of either execution or overall performance. One exception is a Jota built at the factory for the Shah of Iran. Called the SVJ, this was a production Miura

SV modified to have – or so it is understood – a higher-powered engine, a lighter and slightly restyled body, a restyled interior, and such details as an additional oil cooler, a quick-fill fuel cap and a competition exhaust. The car has survived, and remains in Iran in the ownership of a former member of the Shah's inner circle.

The Jota prototype seen from the rear, showing the small spoiler mounted on the tail. It is in the same blood-orange colour favoured by Miura owners; Laverda also used the colour, on their 1,000cc triple-cylinder Jota motorcycle.

Buying Hints

1. The Miura demands a conscientious owner prepared to spend time and money keeping the car up to scratch. Satisfy yourself that this has been the case.

2. The floor and the edges of all panels are likely corrosion black-spots.

3. Budget for expenditure if you buy a Miura – the car is likely to need some work, however good its apparent condition.

4. Very few Miuras come on to the market, and certainly very few good ones, so you'll need to keep your ears to the grapevine: cars often change hands on the basis of word of mouth alone, rather than being advertised.

Above: On the road with the golden Miura S from Lamborghini's own collection. (LAT)

Left: The curve of the side window was a motif seen on Bertone projects during the Giugiaro era. The slats hide the door button. (LAT)

and gearbox on all but the first few cars, and completely revised suspension; a limited-slip differential was another enhancement, as was a leather interior. To accommodate a rear track roughly 5in wider, plus wider rear wheels, the rear wings were flared out, making it easy for those with a keen eye to recognise the SV; at the front, meanwhile, the headlamp 'eyelashes' disappeared in favour of plain black headlamp surrounds. The last of these cars was built in 1972.

On the subject of power outputs, Bob Wallace denies official claims. He says that no production Miura had more than 325bhp and there was never more than 15-20bhp difference between the various models. He also asserts that a good SV will attain 180mph if there is a long enough stretch of road.

Miura production of all types amounted, officially, to 764 cars. Some chassis experts disagree and say that the true number is about 750, because the total of 764 includes rebuilds.

The Islero

If there's such a thing as the forgotten Lamborghini – or indeed the unloved Lamborghini – then the sober-lined 1968–70 Islero wears such a mantle, sandwiched as it is, Cinderella-like, between the curvaceously sixties 400GT and the more outrageous Bertone offerings that seemed so emblematic of the early seventies.

But the Islero, named after the bull that killed famed bullfighter Manuel Rodriguez in 1947, was definitely no aberration: it was a totally logical step forward for the company. Introduced at the early 1968 Geneva show, it was a clever updating of the 400GT 2+2, keeping all that car's mechanicals but wrapping them in a more crisply styled and more

modern body. Lamborghini thus gave a new lease of life to its mainstay product, a sensible move that avoided the risk of over-reliance on the Miura or the future four-seater Espada to bring home the bacon.

Powered by the 400GT's 320bhp version of the 3.9-litre V12, the Islero differed from its predecessor only in having beefed-up anti-roll bars – plus Campagnolo alloy wheels instead of Borrani wires. Shorter by 4.5in than the 400GT 2+2, the Islero was also some 3.6cwt lighter.

The all-steel body with its retractable headlamps was the work of Marazzi, builder of the last 400s, and its style was evolved with input from Ferruccio Lamborghini himself – or so the story goes. Sharp-edged

In all likelihood the first Islero – or one of the very first – the car in this press photograph wears Borrani wires rather than the Campagnolo alloys of regular Isleros.

and conservative, the lines had the cost-saving virtue of dispensing with the double-curvature glass used on the 350/400 models. Inside there was more room at the back, while the squared-off boot gave increased luggage accommodation. The specification included electric windows and air-conditioning – admittedly not very efficient – as standard equipment, and at first glance the interior was impressively plush.

Look closer, though, and it was a pretty amateurish effort, with poor standards of finish and a jumbled mess of switchgear. Marazzi was a small and relatively poorly-equipped company, and simply didn't seem capable of achieving high standards of either internal or external finish: the Touring-built earlier cars were acknowledged at the time to have been far better constructed.

Some improvement was noticeable, all the same, when the original Islero gave way in early 1969 to the Islero S. Immediately recognisable by its flared wheelarches and front-window quarter-lights, the 'S' featured a 350bhp engine and uprated suspension drawing on that of the Espada; equally important, however, was the comprehensively revised interior, which boasted an all-new dashboard and centre console and much improved seating with twin rear buckets. Other details of the 'S' included a more prominent bonnet scoop, horizontal vents in the front wings, and below-bumper foglamps as standard.

In all, a mere 225 Isleros were made, of which 100 were the 'S'; the last car left the factory in April 1970.

The original Islero is recognisable by its plain unflared wheelarches. The slender high-set bumpers are an unusual styling feature. (LAT)

Lamborghini Islero
1968–70

ENGINE:
60-degree V12, front-mounted; aluminium-alloy construction throughout

Capacity	3929cc
Bore x stroke	82mm x 62mm
Valve actuation	Twin overhead camshafts per bank of cylinders, chain-driven
Compression ratio	9.5:1
Carburettors	Six Weber twin-choke 40 DCOE 2V
Power	320bhp (DIN) at 6500rpm 350bhp (DIN) at 7000rpm (Islero S)
Torque	275lb ft at 4500rpm 289lb ft at 5500rpm (Islero S)

TRANSMISSION:
Rear-wheel drive; five-speed Lamborghini-made gearbox with synchromesh on all ratios including reverse; limited-slip differential
Final drive 4.09:1

SUSPENSION:
Front: Independent by coils and unequal-length double wishbones; combined spring/damper units; anti-roll bar
Rear: Independent by coils and unequal-length double wishbones; combined spring/damper units; anti-roll bar

STEERING:
ZF worm-and-sector; no power assistance; 4.3 turns lock-to-lock

BRAKES:
Front: Girling 11.8-inch (300mm) disc
Rear: Girling 11-inch (280mm) disc

WHEELS/TYRES
Cast-alloy centre-lock 15in wheels with triple-eared knock-off hub spinners; 7in rims
Tyres 21 x 15 Pirelli Cinturato HS

BODYWORK:
Two-door 2+2 coupé in aluminium by Marazzi

DIMENSIONS:
Length	14ft 10.1in (4.525m)
Wheelbase	8ft 4.4in (2.65m)
Track, front and rear	4ft 6.3in (1.38m)
Height	4ft 2in (1.27m)

WEIGHT (KERB):
24.96cwt (1,268kg)

PERFORMANCE:
(Source: *Sports Car Graphic*)
Max speed	159mph
0–60mph	7.5sec
0–100mph	13.8sec

NUMBER BUILT:
Islero	125
Islero S	100

Above: The interior of a 1970 Islero S: the velvet plush of the seats is somehow typical of Italian trim of the era. The imitation wood dashboard would cause a Jaguar enthusiast to raise his or her eyebrows; this style is specific to the 'S' version of the Islero. (LAT)

Right: The Islero inherited its running gear from the 400GT; this engine-bay shot is of an 'S'. (LAT)

Opposite: The Islero S is identifiable by its flared wheelarches and its front quarterlights; additionally the bonnet scoop is more prominent and there are horizontal vents in the front wings. The Islero retained the glassiness of the 350/400, but was a much crisper design.

From Monster to Masterpiece: Gavin Sutherland and

Restoring my car has been like a modern version of *The Picture of Dorian Gray*. While I've got older and craggier, my car has got better and better.

I was already a keen classic car enthusiast when I bought my Lamborghini Islero S, at an auction in Scotland, for £12,200. I had noticed its pop-up headlamps: one up and one down. It seemed to be winking at me. I looked under the bonnet at the engine – the saddest sight you could imagine, but still thought 'What a masterpiece. I'll never own a car like that.'

I'm not sure what made me bid for it. The story is a classic tale of someone putting his foot in a small puddle and ending up in water above his head. I was young, naïve, ignorant and stupid. However, if it had fallen into someone else's hands it might not exist now, as most people in the know would have bought it and sold it as parts.

[The] truth of what I had done started to dawn. But I was still keen. It was my money in there and I felt that I was lucky to have the chance to do something with it. I decided to keep the car, and resolved to sell it if things got too difficult. I had already had people offer to buy it, with a view to selling it as parts.

The running bits are early 1960s, with a late 1960s body, and some strange 1970s ideas thrown in, so it didn't ooze sophistication the way the earlier cars did. But everything was the same in terms of the driving, performance and feel of the car.

I was on a mission. I decided to get the running gear going, so that I could drive it. I've never been trained as an engineer, although I know how to undo a nut and bolt, so I contacted Colin Clark, a respected engineer and mentor, for help with the engine. Most people start with a Mini and rebuild it before going on to something else. Not me, I decided to start with a Lamborghini!

Colin told me the frightening facts about the engine and the (huge) projected costs of fixing it. Ten years

of lying in a field had taken its toll, and just about everything that moved in it had to be replaced [or] overhauled.

Next, I decided to repaint the car – or what was left of it that wasn't labelled and sitting beneath its body in boxes. I poured paint stripper over it and realised the horrible truth. It looked like Frankenstein's monster. Every panel on the car had been damaged by an incompetent welder, who had used up to an inch of filler in some places to bring the levels up.

Realising that every single part of the car had to be redone was a real low point. The roof was sagging, the doors were rotten, the list was endless. The work required was

Gavin Sutherland with the Islero that he has so painstakingly and painfully restored. (Martin Pope)

his Islero

beyond me so I persuaded a professional to rebuild the body the following year. He now admits, as an experienced Lamborghini and Maserati specialist, that it was one of the biggest challenges of his career.

During this time, I was mainly self-employed, and worked on it at weekends. I'd take the running gear apart, paint it and replace anything that wasn't working, and rebuild all the electrical ancillaries. When I was out of work, I'd spend all my time on it.

My friends thought I was a nutcase, but I knew the car would have no value unless it was back in one piece. The alternative was selling it as bits. I felt I'd started down a one-way tunnel, and the further I went with the project, the more difficult and perhaps stupid it seemed not to finish.

As time has passed, there have been many, many times when I wished I didn't have it. The car has constantly tested me, but I've always managed to find a way forward with money, or patience, or good fortune, or someone offering to help me out. I've also learned a lot.

There were good times, too, like when all the parts going back into the car were new, rather than old and greasy. I really felt that I was winning then; it was a time when everything fitted together well – the time spent on the car was good and my work and social life were good.

Naturally, the first time I drove it, three years ago, I felt elated. I could only drive to the end of the road, though, as it hadn't passed its MoT.

The low points were discovering the truth about the engine and the shell. Every single panel in the car has been replaced, to the tune of £9,000. I managed to find the panels from Lamborghini themselves, who happened to have them hanging around the back of their warehouse.

I've stopped looking at bills. I really don't know, and don't want to know what I've spent to date. All I know is that the car's got to be finished. I have great fits of enthusiasm with it and then there will be six months when I don't want to see it.

I work on an intuitive basis, and when I run into problems I have to turn to the professionals. Not having engineering experience meant I never really felt confident enough to say 'This is going to be done by then.' I would just accept when it was finished with a sigh of relief and think 'What's next?' I would always give myself a pat on the back for reaching the next point.

My car has taken over my life. I'm not sure that's a good thing, and I think my partner Sharon would agree. As the car approaches completion, and becomes a more valuable asset, if something breaks, I'm faced with a very large bill. The parts alone would cost thousands.

When it's completely finished, I'll have to sell it as I couldn't afford to run it. For every 200 miles, it costs £100 in fuel. The expense of running and keeping these cars is what costs. And you do need to run them, or else keep them pampered in a heated garage. It's a big responsibility, but if I had the money, I think I'd keep it.

I'm not sure I'll be heartbroken to see it go though, although I'll feel a very large part of my life has left me. I am sure I'll feel intensely proud, as well as a big loss, mixed in with relief. It's impossible to say, though. When it happens, I might become a sobbing wreck.

If I could do anything again, I probably wouldn't buy it, even though it's such an exotic motor car. Most of the time, it's been a pleasure to work on. What I will enjoy is seeing the pleasure it gives to the next person. Someone once said to me 'With these cars, you're caretakers, not owners', and I think that's true. Sadly, my time with it may becoming to an end.

© The Telegraph Group Limited

Driving the Islero

On the road the Islero performs as exceptionally as its predecessors. As always, the best feature of the car is the short-stroke V12 four-cam engine, continuing development work having made it smoother than ever. Induction noise from the Weber carburettors is a little subdued by large air-cleaner boxes, but nothing can tame the mechanical noise of chains and valves working hard.

Perfect the Islero is not. It has superbly balanced handling and very high cornering power, but the ZF worm-and-sector steering inherited from the 400GT remains on the low-geared side, and while good for its type does not match the same maker's rack-and-pinion set-up, as fitted to cars such as the Aston Martin. The hefty action of the gearchange and the firm clutch are as the 400GT, and may not please everybody, while the firmer suspension has given the Islero a less supple ride. A more important demerit is that the interior presentation, whether Islero or Islero S, will be judged by many as being sadly lacklustre.

Buying Hints

1. Many poor Isleros have been broken for spares, as restoration has not proved economic. Let this be a salutary warning – as well as an indication that finding a good car in the UK is likely to be difficult.

2. Body corrosion is the Islero's principal weakness – check everywhere. All the usual areas are vulnerable to rust: wheelarches, wing bottoms, door bottoms, sills.

The Espada

To provide adequate seating for four people, a roomy body is essential, but the rear overhang on the Espada is perhaps a little excessive for a high-performance car. This is an early Series II car, still on the original Miura-style Campagnolo alloys.

During the early years of the company, while it was under the control of Ferruccio Lamborghini, there was a conscious effort to put on the market a full range of cars. Accordingly, at the 1968 Geneva motor show the company introduced the Tipo 108 Espada, a full four-seater saloon with exquisitely well-balanced lines. 'Espada' means a sword in Spanish and, despite what has been written elsewhere, does not mean any particular type of sword and has no direct connection with bullfighting. Although there were two cars on display in Switzerland, the press was at first reluctant to accept that the Espada was a production car, as opposed to a special 'motor show' project.

That is understandable, as the Bertone lines of the Espada had clear links to a brace of previous show cars created by the Turin styling house. The most obvious influence for the new model was the flamboyant Marzal produced by Gandini for the 1967 Geneva show: the Espada's profile, wheelarch openings and waistline treatment are pure Marzal. Missing

Lamborghini Espada
1968-78

ENGINE:
60-degree V12, front-mounted; aluminium-alloy construction throughout

Capacity	3929cc
Bore x stroke	82mm x 62 mm
Valve actuation	Twin overhead camshafts per bank of cylinders, chain-driven
Compression ratio	9.5:1
Carburettors	Six Weber twin-choke 40DCOE 20
Power	325bhp at 6500rpm (350bhp from 1970)
Torque	276lb ft at 4500rpm (289lb ft at 5500rpm from 1970)

TRANSMISSION:
Rear-wheel drive; five-speed Lamborghini-made gearbox with synchromesh on all forward gears and reverse; Lamborghini-made hypoid-bevel differential, (Lamborghini limited-slip differential optional) Final drive 4.5:1

SUSPENSION:
Front: Independent by coils and unequal-length double wishbones; combined spring/damper units; anti-roll bar
Rear: Independent by coils and unequal-length double wishbones; combined spring/damper units; anti-roll bar

STEERING:
Worm-and-cam; power assistance optional from 1970 and standard from 1973; 3.8 turns lock-to-lock

BRAKES:
Front: Girling 11.8-inch (300mm) disc
Rear: Girling 11-inch (280mm) disc
Dual circuit; servo assistance

WHEELS/TYRES:
Cast-alloy centre-lock 15in wheels with triple-eared spinners; 7in rims
Tyres 205VR x 15 Pirelli CN72 Cinturato

BODYWORK:
Four-seat, two-door steel saloon by Bertone

DIMENSIONS:

Length	15ft 4in (4.67m)
Wheelbase	8ft 8.3in (2.60m)
Track, front and rear	4ft 10.6in (1.49m)
Width	5ft 11.7in (1.82m)
Height	3ft 10.9in (1.19m)

WEIGHT (KERB):
29.1cwt (1,480kg)

PERFORMANCE:
(Source: *Road & Track*)

Max speed	158mph
0-60mph	6.5sec
0-100mph	15.8sec

PRICE INCLUDING TAX WHEN NEW:
£10,900 (1971)

NUMBER MADE:
1217

Above: The Jaguar Pirana, based on the E-type 2+2, clearly shares its frontal treatment with the Espada. (Bertone)

Left: A rear view of the Pirana also shows many similarities, not least in the upward sweep of the rear side-window. (Bertone)

Next two pages: These overhead views emphasise the smooth outline of Bertone's body for the Espada and shows the NACA ducts in the front wings . . . while from the rear the sizeable exposed luggage area is visible.

Driving the Espada

No one has criticised the performance and stability of the Espada. Tractable at low revs, creamily muscular in its seamless acceleration from 4000rpm upwards, the melodious Lamborghini V12 with its howling four cams never fails to seduce. The Espada's handling is similarly superb, with a high level of grip under all conditions and a reassuring feel of safety on streaming wet roads. It is remarkably quiet for such a high-performance car, too, mainly due to the refinement of the V12 engine, but also to excellent soundproofing. The Espada also benefits from the all-Lamborghini transmission, which is remarkably free from whines and vibrations. The gearchange is excellent, with short movements and a very light action, but the steering is very heavy at low speeds on cars not fitted with power assistance – although this vastly improves at higher speeds. Power-steered cars thankfully combine lightness with precision.

It should be pointed out, however,

that although these cars tended to appeal to more mature buyers, there is very little concession to the generally lesser mobility of such people, and despite the width of the doors it is a bit of a struggle for older passengers to get into the back seats. Still, with the spare wheel hidden beneath the boot, there is unobstructed luggage space and plenty of it.

With excellent braking and those superb (for their time) Pirelli CN72 Cinturato tyres, the Espada is, in

Bulky four-seater though it may be, the Espada apologises to nobody when it comes to performance: a maximum speed of close on 160mph is achievable. (LAT)

overall terms, an exceptional 'businessman's express' – provided that you can pardon a fuel consumption of 12–15mpg. It is a genuinely successful attempt to build a full four-seater supercar saloon – a trick that arguably nobody else has pulled off.

from the Espada, of course, are the Marzal's extraordinary fully-glazed gullwing doors, but the initial Espada mock-up did feature a toned-down and less glassy pair of gullwings, before reality set in and orthodox side-hinged doors were written into the specification. This occasioned a re-think of the glasshouse arrangements, and here the second show-car influence surfaced, when Bertone cross-pollinated the Marzal profile with the glasshouse of the 1967 Jaguar Pirana styling exercise. Indeed, according to author Pete Lyons the prototype Espada was shaped on the Pirana's wooden body buck.

One of the most successful of early Lamborghinis, selling steadily over a ten-year period, the Espada differed little in its mechanicals from the 350GT/400GT and from the Islero that appeared the same year. Thus the engine was the usual V12

four-overhead-camshaft all-alloy 3,929cc unit, and with its six twin-choke horizontal Weber carburettors; power output was 325bhp at 6,500rpm – a mere 5bhp less than that developed by the Islero, but 25bhp less than the output of the same engine in the Miura.

The transmission was also almost identical to that of the Islero, with Lamborghini's own gearbox and final-drive unit, but this time the limited-slip differential was optional. Where the Espada differed, however, was in having a completely new design of chassis. Although the company described it as 'unit construction', it would be more accurate to call it a punt-type underframe. Key features were a square-section tubular structure ahead of the scuttle to provide engine, suspension and steering mounts, and what has been described as the

'skeleton' of the pressed-steel wheelarches.

The wheelbase was extended and so as to provide adequate space for four passengers the engine and gearbox were moved almost eight inches forward from the front wheel centre-line. Extending forward from the wheel centre-line were rigid tubular forks that carried the radiator, brake servos and the air-conditioning. The scuttle was a torsionally rigid box-section and the platform centre-section had the usual stiffening propshaft tunnel and sills. Beneath the floor at the rear, another square tubular section served as the mounting for the final-drive casing and the rear suspension. The rear wheelarches and the spare wheel recess provided additional torsional rigidity.

Coil-spring front and rear suspension was by unequal-length wishbones, combined spring/damper

Left: The ornate original interior, with its octagonal-motif instrument binnacle and an equally stylised steering wheel not found on production cars; the row of toggle switches is very Jaguar-ish. (LAT)

Below: This production Espada SI has rocker switches and another – again very mannered – style of steering wheel. (LAT)

Right: The interior of later Espadas is finished to a much higher standard than that of earlier cars, but the light leather is inevitably delicate and soon shows scuff-marks. This is the dashboard of a Series II car – a much tidier effort than Gandini's original.

Below: Bertone produced a particular smooth and harmonious style for the Espada and although buyers of supercars mainly preferred coupés, the Espada sold steadily at a little over 100 cars a year.

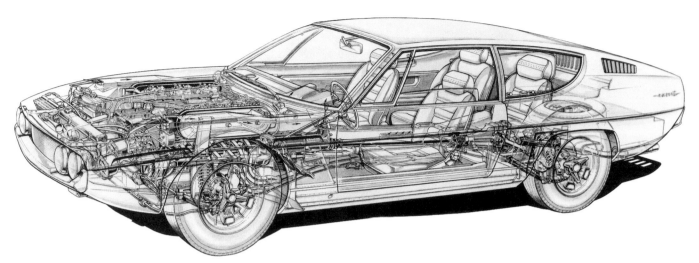

Above: A fascinating and revealing cutaway of the Espada by renowned artist Vic Berris. Apart from the exposé of technical details, this drawing reveals the carefully planned layout of the interior so as to provide more than adequate accommodation for four people. (LAT)

Below: The bonnet of the Espada incorporates the upper section of the front wings, making access easier than on preceding models. (LAT)

units and an anti-roll bar – in other words pretty much as the Islero, although set up to give a sofer ride. The steering remained ZF worm-and-sector and initially power assistance was not available. As was usual on the cars from Sant'Agata, there were Girling disc brakes front and rear with separate circuits.

A lot of the work on the Espada was sub-contracted; after Marchesi, a chassis constructor based in Modena, had completed the chassis and welded underframe, this was transported to Bertone for the steel body with its alloy bonnet to be fitted. The car was then returned to Sant'Agata where it joined the separate Espada production line and the mechanical components were installed.

Because the Espada was just 3ft 11in high yet a massive 5ft 11.7in wide, it looked much bigger than it was. A distinctive feature of the styling was the tumblehome curvature of the side panels, the result of using curved side glass. A strictly horizontal roofline ensured that there was

headroom for two adults in the rear and that there was more than adequate legroom. The bonnet was front-hinged and the front and rear bumpers were purely cosmetic.

The interior was light and airy, with an enormous double-curvature windscreen with twin wipers of the type commonly known as 'clap hands', as they move from the outer edges inwards. At the rear the rather shallow window served as the hatch giving access to the boot. There were bucket seats at the front and rear, so only four people could be carried. As usual with Lamborghinis, the instrumentation, if not well laid-out, was at least very comprehensive.

In the early days the finish was poor and heavily criticized. 'The most disappointing thing about the whole car was the poor workmanship that showed up in various spots, primarily the interior', commented American magazine *Road & Track* when in 1969 it tested a privately-owned Espada. 'There were bad edges, loose panels, a practically useless speedometer calibrated in km/h but with an

odometer reading miles, unfinished and misaligned holes in the front seatbacks, and the like. We appreciate the pitfalls of hand labour, but would think a price of $21,000 allows sufficient time to do the job right.'

When Denis Jenkinson borrowed an Espada from the British concessionaires in 1972, he too commented adversely. 'This was not a new car, it had over 10,000 miles on the odometer, and the quality of the paintwork left something to be desired, the all-steel body-cum-chassis unit showing nasty rust pittings already, which made the detailed instructions [for] touching-up the Thermoplastic Acyrlic 'Duracryl' paintwork all the more poignant', he reported.

In 1970 Lamborghini introduced the Series II or 400 GTE version of the Espada, with a more powerful 350bhp engine, optional power steering, and ventilated discs for the brakes. There was also a lowered floor to increase rear headroom, and a much neater interior with the somewhat contrived hex-motif dashboard replaced by a tidier if more conventional layout.

Buying Hints

1. The quality of construction of the bodies was not high, and in those days Italian manufacturers failed to understand rustproofing. Thus although a large number of Espadas were built, many have rusted themselves into oblivion. It is not so much a question of where to start looking for rust, it is more a question of where to stop. The wheelarches, sills, A-pillars, lower front wings and the bottoms of the doors are all highly vulnerable. Replacement panels are of course not available, but specialists can provide repair sections or secondhand replacements that have been re-made.

2. The Espada is one of the few cars where even the roof rusts. Check around the vents let into the rear

edge of the roof. If there is evidence of water entering the interior via the headlining, the drain tubes in the roof bracing traverse are likely to have blocked, causing the box to rot through and allow water into the car. The roof is also prone to denting.

3. Although the bonnet is alloy, electrolytic reaction with its steel frame may have caused corrosion at the edges.

4. Chrome fittings are scarce and expensive. The interior trim was not of high quality and will almost certainly need replacing or refurbishing.

5. The heart of every Lamborghini is its engine and gearbox. Some experts say that if the engine has a smoky

exhaust, it indicates worn exhaust guides. In my more limited experience, however, I have never known – even when they were in the prime – early Lamborghinis that did not smoke a little. The answer is if the car is sound in other respects, have the engine fully examined before making a decision.

6. Despite its bulk, the Espada should handle crisply. If the steering feels dead and does not self-centre, worn bushing could have put the front end out of alignment. A car that wallows or wanders is likely to be suffering from worn and/or out-of-adjustment suspension.

7. Beware a car needing a new exhaust system; these are hugely expensive.

In a solid colour such as red the Espada takes on a different character. This is a Series III model. (LAT)

One of Lamborghini's main concerns at this time was to meet United States Federal emission requirements. In 1969 the company had set up a special office headed by Ing Antonio Catanzano with a view to 'detoxing' the Espada and Jarama models. This was achieved by using an air pump with special carburettor and ignition settings. The Espada passed the Federal regulations on 31 December 1969 and thereafter Lamborghini supplied special versions to United States requirements. Certain American regulations affected makers whose production exceeded 500 cars a year, but as Lamborghini production amounted to only 473 cars in 1969, the company enjoyed a level of exemption.

A third series of Espada arrived in 1973, with power steering and air-con as standard, a further revised dashboard, and modified brakes and suspension. The following year automatic transmission was offered, this being the three-speed Chrysler TorqueFlite as also used on the Chrysler-powered Bristol and Jensen. Although the Lamborghini V12 was more flexible than others of this configuration, it was less than satisfactory to use such a high-performance engine with an automatic gearbox. Only seven automatic cars were built and almost all were exported to the United States.

Marzal: The Showcar Stunner

The Marzal rates as one of the legendary show cars of the sixties, being sufficiently emblematic to have become a long-lived Matchbox toy – always a reasonable guide, in those days, to a design's 'pin-up' status!

Only 3ft 7.3in high, the Marzal's key feature was a single, very wide, gullwing door each side, glazed in two panels down to sill level and moving through 115 degrees. There was also a large glass panel in the roof, but other than two hinged quarterlights there were no opening windows, so not only were the driver and passengers fully exposed to onlookers, but they were also generously exposed to the sun. Thankfully, then, the Marzal was fully air-conditioned – although this probably would not have helped very much, because European systems of the time, especially that used by Lamborghini, were notoriously inefficient.

Another feature was the rear window, which had slatting that repeated the hexagonal honeycomb motifs of the interior and was designed both to admit light to the interior and draw in air to cool the engine. Although the slatting was not to surface on the Espada, the hexagonal motif did end up being used for the production car's dashboard.

Substantially the work of Marcello Gandini, the Marzal was based on a platform chassis with an 8ft 8.3in wheelbase, offering seating for four. The power unit was a 1,997cc V6, effectively one half of the usual 3,929cc V12 Lamborghini engine, and was mounted transversely behind the rear axle line and inclined at an angle of 30 degrees to the front of the car; output was claimed as 175bhp at 6,800rpm. Transmission was by the usual Lamborghini five-speed gearbox and the radiator was

mounted at the rear. As a result of this, there was space at the front for a 21-gallon fuel tank with adequate luggage room above. Apart from the aluminium-alloy panel over the fuel tank at the front, the body was of all-steel construction.

Top: With its midships engine the Marzal has a lower bonnet line; otherwise its profile is very similar to that of the Espada. (Bertone)

Above: The gullwing doors are the dominant styling feature, and are accompanied by a glass roof panel. (Bertone)

Top: Extraordinary silvered upholstery makes the interior as striking as the exterior; the car is a genuine four-seater. Middle: All hatches open! The clamshell bonnet found its way onto the Espada. Bottom: The sci-fi dashboard uses – to excess? – the hexagonal motif found on the rear slatting. Left: Unusual up-high shot emphasises that the glasshouse is just that. (Bertone)

The Jarama

Introduced in 1970 to replace the Islero, the Jarama was the last front-engined Lamborghini. Viewed with a little height, the characteristic NACA ducts are clearly visible.

Another new model arrived in 1970, this being the 2+2 Jarama with occasional rear seats. Intended to replace the Islero, the new car was first seen at the Geneva show that March and was to be the last front-engined Lamborghini. It was named after the Spanish town near Madrid, famous for its fighting bulls for more than a century.

The tubular chassis of the Islero was

Lamborghini Jarama

1970-78

ENGINE:
60-degree V12, front-mounted; aluminium-alloy construction throughout

Capacity	3929cc
Bore x stroke	82mm x 62mm
Valve actuation	Twin overhead camshafts per bank of cylinders, chain-driven
Compression ratio	10.7:1
Carburettors	Six Weber twin-choke 40DCOE
Power	350bhp (DIN) at 7500rpm
	365bhp (DIN) at 7500rpm (Jarama S)
Torque	289lb ft at 5500rpm
	300lb ft at 5500rpm (Jarama S)

TRANSMISSION:
Rear-wheel drive; five-speed Lamborghini-made gearbox with synchromesh on all forward gears and reverse; limited-slip differential
Final drive 4.09:1

SUSPENSION:
Front: Independent by coil springs and unequal-length wishbones; Koni telescopic dampers; anti-roll bar
Rear: Independent by coil springs and unequal-length wishbones; Koni telescopic dampers; anti-roll bar

STEERING:
Worm-and-cam ; no power assistance; 4.3 turns lock-to-lock

BRAKES:
Front: Girling 11.8in (300mm) ventilated disc
Rear: Girling 11.0in (280mm) ventilated disc
Dual circuit; servo assistance

WHEELS/TYRES:
Cast-alloy centre-lock 15in wheels;
7in rims.
Tyres 215-70VR Michelin X radial-ply

BODYWORK:
Two-door 2+2 fixed-head coupé; steel frame, alloy panels. Designed by Bertone, constructed by Marazzi

DIMENSIONS:

Length	14ft 7in (4.445m)
Wheelbase	7ft 9.6in (2.40m)
Track, front	4ft 10.5in (1.485m);
Track, rear	4ft 11in (1,50m)
Width	6ft 0in (1.83m)
Height	3ft 11.5in (1.205m)

WEIGHT (KERB):
31.0cwt (1575kg)

PERFORMANCE:
(Source: *Motor*)

Max speed	162mph
0-60mph	6.8sec
0-100mph	16.4sec
30-50mph in top	8.8sec
50-70mph in top	8.0sec

PRICE INCLUDING TAX WHEN NEW:
£8,958 (1971); air-conditioning £280 extra; metallic paint £220 extra

NUMBER MADE:

Jarama	177
Jarama S	150

replaced by one of steel platform-type, in effect, a shortened version of that used on the Espada. While the longer Espada had a 50:50 weight distribution, that of the Jarama was 52:48 front-to-rear. Once again Bertone's Gandini was responsible for the styling, which developed themes seen on his more ornate Iso Lele revealed the previous year; students of artistic continuity will also find many similarities with the special-bodied Fiat 128 that Bertone also presented in 1969. The bodies continued to be built by Marazzi, but from pressings supplied by Bertone.

Although the curve of the nose arguably clashed with the angularity of the rear window line, the Jarama was a very neat design, with flared wheelarches, curved side windows, and an upward kick in the roofline to meet the very steeply raked rear window. An unusual feature – also found on the Lele – was that the four quartz-halogen headlamps were partially shielded, the clamshell covers dropping down courtesy an electric motor. This enabled Bertone to create a strong frontal appearance, with a straight line across the car at the leading edge of the bonnet and a very shallow air-intake,

The cockpit of a Jarama S: the effect is workmanlike if a little drab, with all that dark grey suede. (LAT)

Driving the Jarama

On the road the Jarama remains a magnificent experience, coloured above all by that superb V12. But relative to the Islero it is bigger, heavier and softer – and that shows.

On lesser roads the car's bulk makes itself felt, and cars with manual steering have slightly slower responses – as well as a fair amount of weight at the helm at low speeds and when parking.

The Jarama also has a bit more understeer when cornered fast, while the ride is a degree softer. More civilised, a touch less incisive, the Jarama still has a huge reserve of abilities, whether we're talking of performance or roadholding. The model's greatest qualities are its ability to cruise effortlessly at 130mph, and the way the back end digs in under hard acceleration as you power through corners – all this supported by the disdainful efficiency of the car's magnificent Girling disc brakes.

If lighting up the rear tyres is your sort of game, the Jarama has power a-plenty to oblige – as this Lamborghini test-driver demonstrates.

supplemented by twin NACA ducts on the bonnet to feed air to the interior ventilation system.

Luggage accommodation was wide but shallow, with more luggage accommodation available by folding down the rear occasional seats. Compared with earlier front-engined Lamborghinis, the switchgear in the central console was much simpler and another improvement was in the paint finish, which was in general superior to that of the Islero. But while the interior was in the usual high-quality leather, there was also the usual indifferent workmanship.

Minor criticisms were that drivers, especially those of shorter stature, looked mainly through the bottom of the windscreen and the view was marred by the parked windscreen wipers; this became particularly irritating on left-hand corners. Seen through the windscreen, the bonnet appeared as a bland expanse of metal that made it difficult to judge the width of the Jarama, which at 6ft made it a very wide car by European standards.

Early cars had the 350bhp engine,

Above: The bonnet scoop – and the five-stud wheels – identify this Jarama as an 'S' version; only 150 were built.

Left: For a 2+2, luggage space is adequate, as this Motor *road-test shot demonstrates. (LAT)*

Opposite: There is a certain brutalism about the front-on view. Lamborghini was rather over-fond of poorly integrated add-on auxiliary lamps.

Bertone: Coachbuilder to Lamborghini

Nuccio Bertone, 1914–1997, became one of the greatest Italian coachbuilders and, along with Pininfarina and Zagato, Carrozzeria Bertone is one of the few long-established coachbuilding houses to have survived to this day.

Nuccio Bertone's father, Giovanni, was the founder of the company. He had been born into a farming family in 1884, and after learning the trades of woodworking and metalworking for horse-drawn carriages he moved to Turin at the age of 23, married, and set up his own business. He gradually progressed from horse-drawn carriages to horseless carriages, but he always remained a skilled artisan rather than a stylist.

There was a strong demand for competent, able coachbuilders, who could work efficiently, quickly and cheaply. Work came in from Ceirano, Chiribiri, FAST, Fiat, Itala and SCAT, and Bertone soon moved from his original small premises to workshops twice the size and with 20 employees.

Giovanni Bertone developed a close working relationship with the Lancia company and during the 1920s most of his work was on this Turin company's chassis. During the 1930s Nuccio Bertone joined his father's company and acted primarily as salesman, while Giovanni dealt with the orders. Orders were hard to come by, but the company managed to stay financially solvent.

When Mussolini embarked on Italy's rearmament programme, there was no shortage of orders or income and the coachbuilding industry enjoyed a boom, building bodies for military vehicles and diversifying into aircraft components.

Nuccio Bertone became general manager in 1950 and, despite a shortage of work, he saw a way forward for the company if it was able to secure orders for the manufacture in series of cars with Bertone coachwork. The first breakthrough

Nuccio Bertone, longtime head of the Bertone coachbuilding concern. (Photo courtesy Bertone 90 Years 1912>2002 – Stile Industria Design)

came in 1952 when he secured an order from American dealer S H 'Wacky' Arnolt to build at first bodies for MGs and subsequently Bristols for the United States market. In all, 103 bodies were built on the MG TD chassis, and 142 Bertone-bodied Arnolt-Bristols.

During the 1950s Nuccio Bertone collaborated closely with Alfa Romeo and built the bizarrely styled BAT (*Berlina Aerodinamica Tecnica*) series of cars with experimental aerodynamic bodies, the aim of which was to increase downforce on the rear of the bodywork by the use of channels and fins.

At the same time Bertone also built

a limited number of bodies on Alfa Romeo and Ferrari chassis, and the big breakthrough came when Bertone built the prototype Giulietta Sprint body. This entered production in Bertone's works and over a period of ten years some 34,000 were built. Bertone moved to new and much larger premises in 1958, and by 1961 the company had 800 employees, had automated production lines and was building 10,000 units annually. Bertone was responsible for many later Alfa Romeo bodies, including the 1750GTV and 2000GTV and the immensely popular GT Junior.

Another move to a larger factory was made in 1963 and from 1965 onwards Bertone built the bodies for Fiat 850 Spiders: by the time the model was withdrawn in 1972, production of these little sports cars had amounted to around 140,000 vehicles. Another very successful project was the mid-engined Fiat X1/9 sports car, once described as a mini-Ferrari, that Bertone built at the rate of 150 a week.

Nuccio Bertone was joined by his brother-in-law Tiberio Gracco, who was put in charge of production. Bertone always encouraged the young who had flair and in the 1960s the average age of the company's employees was only 25. Among the successful stylists who worked for the company were Giorgio Giugiaro and Marcello Gandini – the latter being responsible for the Countach.

When Carrozzeria Touring failed, Bertone was Lamborghini's almost automatic choice. Neither Touring nor Bertone had worked with Ferrari for some years, so there was no possibility of conflict with Maranello. Today Bertone continues to build specialist bodies for mass-manufacturers and one of the company's most successful projects in recent years has been the drophead coupé version of the Fiat Punto.

*No surprises under the bonnet of a Jarama:
this is a 1973-made 'S', which means there's
360bhp at the driver's disposal, thanks to
better manifolding and warmer cams. (LAT)*

but the Jarama S of 1972 onwards was
to almost Miura tune, with power
boosted to 365bhp. Maximum speed
rose from 160mph to about 165mph.
Spot one of these later cars by its
shallow central air scoop on the
bonnet, and the black vents in the
front wings. The bumpers are also
different, with those at the front
having larger indicators set into the
blades, while the alloy wheels changed
to those found on later Espadas.

Although the Jarama also
remained in production until 1978,
demand never took off and the cars
were built in only very small
numbers. The model was simply not
dramatic enough in appearance to
represent properly that it was a very
exceptional high-performance car.
Today, Jaramas represent another
Lamborghini 'snip' – or a pig in poke –
depending on whether you are an
optimist or a pessimist.

Of the total production run of 327
cars, about 12 with right-hand drive
came to the UK and, of course, not all
survived. So if you want a Jarama, it
will probably be lhd or nothing.

Buying Hints

1. Previous warnings about body
corrosion apply equally to the
Jarama – buying a car from a
warmer country outside the UK,
where salt is not used on the
roads, is a sensible idea.

2. Mechanically, too, previous
remarks apply. Again, a sloppiness
to the car's handling indicates
worn suspension bushing and/or
tired dampers.

The Urraco

If Lamborghini's plans had worked out, the Urraco would have transformed the company into a producer of cars in far greater numbers. However, financial problems and poor quality control meant that the company sold substantially fewer of the baby Lamborghini than expected.

Opposite: The Urraco's body was again the work of Bertone and is very neatly styled and well balanced, although the shuttering extending from the sides at the rear across the back of the car is of debatable merit.

Ever since Lamborghini had appeared on the motoring scene, there had been rumours of a smaller-capacity car. But it was not until the Turin show in late 1970 that a new small Lamborghini was finally unveiled – and even then production took some good time get underway. The new 2.5-litre model was called the Urraco, after a breed of fighting bull, and broke new ground for the company in having a 90-degree V8 engine. It also marked an important stage in the technical evoution of Lamborghini cars: from now onwards all new models would have the engine mounted at the rear.

The Urraco was conceived as a rival

to the Ferrari Dino and the Porsche 911, but inevitably it proved more expensive than originally planned and far fewer were sold than anticipated. Delays in getting the car into production didn't help: before manufacture could begin a factory extension had to be completed and full production did not get under way until 1973, by which time the company had come under Swiss control.

Five Urraco prototypes were built and development work resulted in a large number of changes to the design: the first car had been built in a hurry, apparently in less than nine months, and was far from fit for

Urraco P200/P250
1972–79

ENGINE:
90-degree V8, mid-mounted transversely; aluminium-alloy construction throughout

Capacity	2463cc
	1994cc (P200)
Bore x stroke	86mm x 53mm
	74.4mm x 53mm (P200)
Valve actuation	Single overhead camshaft per bank of cylinders, belt-driven
Compression ratio	10.4:1
Carburettors	Four twin-choke downdraught Weber 40IFDF 1
Power	220bhp (DIN) at 7500rpm
	182bhp (DIN) at 7500rpm (P200)
Torque	166lb ft at 5750rpm
	130lb ft at 3800rpm (P200)

TRANSMISSION:
Rear-wheel drive; five-speed Lamborghini-made gearbox with synchromesh on all forward gears and reverse
Final drive 4.25:1

SUSPENSION:
Front: MacPherson struts, lower links; anti-roll bar
Rear: MacPherson struts, reversed lower wishbones; anti-roll bar

STEERING:
Rack-and-pinion; no power assistance; four turns lock-to-lock

BRAKES:
Front: Girling 10.9-inch (275mm) ventilated disc
Rear: Girling 10.9-inch (275mm) ventilated disc
Dual circuit; no servo assistance

WHEELS/TYRES:
Campagnolo cast magnesium-alloy 14in wheels; five-stud fixing; 7.5-inch rims
Tyres 205/70 VR14 Michelin XWX radial-ply

BODYWORK:
Two-door 2+2 coupé in steel, by Bertone

DIMENSIONS:

Length	13ft 11.2in (4.25m)
Wheelbase	8ft 0.5in (2.45m)
Track, front and rear	4ft 9.5in (1.46m)
Width	5ft 9.3in (1.76m)
Height	3ft 7.7in (1.11m)

WEIGHT (KERB):
25.75cwt (1,308kg)

PERFORMANCE:
(Source: *Autocar*)

Max speed	143mph
0–60mph	8.5sec
0–100mph	23sec
30–50mph in top	10.4sec
50–70mph in top	10.7sec

PRICE INCLUDING TAX WHEN NEW:
£9,385 (1974)

NUMBER MADE:

P200	77
P250	520

Urraco P300
1974–79

As P250, except:

ENGINE:

Capacity	2997cc
Bore x stroke	86mm x 64.5mm
Valve actuation	Twin overhead camshafts per bank of cylinders, chain-driven
Carburettors	Four twin-choke downdraught Weber 40DCNF
Power	250bhp (DIN) at 7500rpm
Torque	166.3lb ft at 5750rpm

TRANSMISSION:
Final drive 4.0:1

WEIGHT (KERB):
26.7cwt (1,356kg)

PERFORMANCE:
(Source: *Motor*)

Max speed	158mph
0–60mph	7.6sec
0–100mph	17.5sec
30–50mph in top	9.1sec
50–70mph in top	8.2sec

PRICE INCLUDING TAX WHEN NEW:
£10,545 (1975)

NUMBER MADE:
190

It was the fashion in the 1970s to photograph Lamborghinis with doors, front boot, engine cover and rear boot open. (LAT)

production. Not least, in its original form the engine proved insufficiently powerful to comply with anti-pollution legislation without substantial loss of performance. This was solved and eventually there were to be three different versions of the power unit. Many other detail changes, including the style and standard of trim and an improved air-conditioning system, were made during the development period.

Heart of the Urraco was the new 2,463cc V8, an all-alloy unit with a single overhead camshaft per bank of cylinders; unprecedentedly for Lamborghini, the camshafts were driven by belt rather than by chain. Delivering 220bhp, the engine was mounted transversely behind the driving compartment and, because of its compactness, to the right of the centre-line of the car. To the left of the

engine and alongside it was the five-speed gearbox.

A pinion on the secondary shaft drove a straight-cut spur crownwheel in the differential casing mounted immediately behind the gearbox. The result of this arrangement was that the driveshafts were of unequal length and pointed forwards at an angle of ten degrees. The longer shaft, on the right-hand side, passed between the engine cylinder block and the exhaust manifold of the rear cylinder block. Although this sounds like an unsatisfactory arrangement, it gave no trouble in practice.

The chassis was a sheet-steel semi-monocoque with the engine and gearbox carried in a rubber-insulated subframe with the rear suspension. This arrangement enabled the complete engine and gearbox to be removed from the car as a single unit. Suspension front and rear was by MacPherson struts, with lower links and exceptionally long spring/damper units. This very compact system was

one favoured by Ford and other builders of mundane cars and had not previously been adopted on a very high-performance car. But as a result of careful development it worked, and was one aspect of the car that received very little criticism during the Urraco's production life.

Rack-and-pinion steering was fitted and, unusually, this had no column as such, for the rack was bolted to the scuttle and had very long steering arms. During development-testing there were problems with bump-steer that proved difficult to overcome, but these were eventually cured and this was another aspect of the Urraco that proved complaint-free. There were the usual massive Girling ventilated disc brakes and the wheels were new 7.5in wide-rim 14in-diameter Campagnolo mag-alloys with a five-stud fixing. Mechanically, the Urraco was an exceptional package and it was well matched by the superbly styled Bertone coupé body. In many respects, it was a typical Bertone

Bravo: the 'New Urraco' that never was

The Bravo was a styling exercise by Bertone, unveiled at the 1974 Turin show. Based on the Urraco P300, only with a shortened wheelbase, its wedge-shaped body was in some ways a miniaturised and cleaned-up version of that of the Countach, and featured that car's upward-slashed rear wheelarches – although not its scissor-action doors. Created by Gandini, two aspects of the Bravo were particularly striking: the all-black glazing treatment which had the effect of making the screen pillars disappear, and the complex arrangement of vents for the rear window and the bonnet. The latter were notably unusual, the solid expanses of rectangular slats covering the rear window being mirrored by an identical grid of slats forming the entire bonnet panel. The Bravo was a fully functioning prototype, and it seems that it was a serious study for a future Urraco replacement: it covered over 40,000 miles before retirement.

Above: The slatting on the Bravo's bonnet echoes that at the rear – an unhappy detail. The glasshouse with its concealed pillars is certainly dramatic, though. (Bertone)

Below: The rear view of the Bravo shows off the clean basic lines and the elaborate vents that so reduce rear vision. The square light blocks have a certain affinity with the arrowhead units on the Countach, whose rear wheelarch shape the Bravo also shares. (Bertone)

The prototype Urraco interior, by Bertone, featured a somewhat sparse dashboard with a central binnacle, and a severely dished wheel that looked as if it had been borrowed from a speedboat. (LAT)

wedge-shaped style with covered retractable headlamps, but the most striking feature was the slats running from behind the rear side windows and across the tail. A glass panel separated the rear of the passenger compartment from the engine.

There were two rear lids, the first a slatted cover over the engine and the second, behind it, giving access to the limited luggage accommodation. The combination of the horizontal slats and the vertical support eliminated the chance of seeing much at all in the driving mirror and made reversing difficult.

The interior was very close-coupled, with incredibly cramped rear seats without legroom (the classic 'legless children' arrangement), but the quality of the trim, especially on the leather-

Driving the Urraco

A different breed of Lamborghini the Urraco might be, but on the road it is no less seductive, with limpet-like roadholding, strong braking, and a high-revving little V8 with instantly crisp responses. The negative side of the equation is that neither the gearchange nor the steering are perfect.

The two-shaft gearbox with Porsche synchromesh has the old Zuffenhausen layout with first to the left and down, reverse ahead of it and second to fifth gears in the normal H-layout. The gearlever movement is too long and the change from first to second slow and uncertain; it also makes for a difficult slice across the gate from fourth to third, the change most needed for overtaking. Not helping, the clutch is surprisingly heavy.

As for the steering, that suffers from being too low-geared, a consistent Lamborghini failing on cars made before Sant'Agata offered power-assisted steering. At speed, though, this is not really noticeable, the steering's lightness and precision coming to the fore.

Finally, although vision through the windscreen is excellent, aided by a fairly short bonnet, the view to the rear is notably poor, thanks to those functionally dubious slats.

But if the Urraco has its weak points – and those include a useless handbrake – it also has a dose of the Lamborghini magic: smooth rev-hungry power delivery, massive cornering power and a taut chassis are not negligible virtues. Somehow one feels its promise was not fulfilled, as the company struggled to survive.

The production dashboard is a more orthodox affair, putting the instruments around the wheel and angling the speedo and rev-counter towards the driver. The suede covering is typical of Lamborghinis of the era. (LAT)

upholstered 'S' cars, was much superior to previous Lamborghini efforts. Gone too was the central console with its confusing array of switches and instruments: switchgear was neatly arranged along the dashboard, and both the speedometer and tachometer were clearly visible. Ingeniously, a system of ventilation ducts formed part of the structure.

The 1974 Turin show saw the P250 joined by a 2,997cc P300. Delivering 250bhp at 7,500rpm and a maximum torque of 195lb ft at 3,500rpm, the new 3-litre engine marked a return to quad-cam valve actuation, with drive to the camshafts by chain rather than by the sometimes troublesome belts of the P250 engine. In 1975 a third engine size arrived, primarily for the Italian market: this was a 1,994cc unit said to have a power output of 182bhp, and enabled the resultant Urraco P200 to fit into Italy's under-2,000cc car-tax bracket. Similarly Ferrari built a 2-litre version of the V8 Dino and Maserati offered a 2-litre

version of the Merak; for Lamborghini's contender a maximum speed of 132mph was claimed. Both the P250 and the P300 were available in 'S' form with leather seats and trim, electrically-operated windows and tinted glass.

The Urraco's strongest points were its superb cornering and exceptionally high performance. Overall fuel consumption worked out at around 18mpg for a 2.5-litre car and 15mpg for a 3-litre. A Porsche 911 was a very practical high-performance car suitable for everyday use by reasonably well-heeled motorists; in contrast the Urraco was more a weekend fun car, as it was very tiring over long distances.

The introduction of smaller-capacity, lower-priced cars, still – hopefully – with a healthy profit margin, had been the obvious, commonsense way forward for Lamborghini at the time. But it all went sadly awry. The Urraco spent too long in development, and was not as

reliable or as well-built as the faster versions of the long-established and highly revered Porsche 911 – and in the UK, for example, the P250 Urraco was around £2,500 more expensive than the Porsche 911S and £1,500 more than the Maserati Merak. Nor did buyers, quite rightly, trust in it as fuss-free, everyday transport.

Although the Urraco remained available until 1979, throughout almost all its production life Lamborghini was in financial trouble; consequently production was erratic, quality-control poor and marketing almost non-existent. A production total of 767 over such a long period compares badly with the 2,921 Ferrari 308GTBs built between 1975 and 1981 and the 1,832 Maserati Meraks rolled out in the 1972-83 period.

Athon: another controversial show car

Above: A radical take on an open-top Urraco-based car was the Athon concept car from 1980. (Bertone)

Left: The difficulty of making an elegant job of a fully open car based on a long-decked mid-engine configuration is clearly evident. (Bertone)

Below left: The 'technical' aspect of the Athon's design is most obviously reflected in the hatches set into the rear deck. (Bertone)

Below: Yes, we are back in the early 1980s, of that there's no doubt! The LCD dashboard displays and the square styling motifs are typical of the time. (Bertone)

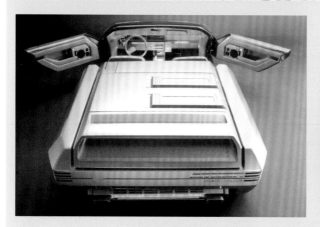

One of the more discussed exhibits at the 1980 Turin show was a styling exercise by Bertone, called the Athon. Based on the Urraco, it was the work of Marc Deschamps, the ex-Renault stylist who had joined Bertone as principal designer the previous year; he was to go on to originate the lines of the Citroën XM, amongst other vehicles, before running the studio of French coachbuilder Heuliez.
Described by Bertone as a 'mechanical' design, the technological look of the Athon was supposedly inspired by cars in science-fiction films and its geometric lines were dominated by a flat rear deck with rectangular access hatches. Other striking features were the deep sills that kicked up into vent panels forward of the rear wheels, and the panoramic windscreen. The interior was equally radical, with a brutalist rectangular theme and LCD instruments – all very early-'80s.

'Some people think it looks like an armoured car or a mobile rocket launcher; other people think it looks beautiful,' reported an evidently bemused *Autocar* magazine. Bertone felt constrained to explain the car's rationale. 'We have deliberately gone to extremes,' it explained to the press. 'For people who for years have been cooped up in cosy sound-proofed boxes, driving a Spider is an intoxicating experience. Total immersion in the wind, an almost tactile sensation of speed, a full view of every situation, lead the driver to behave more cautiously. He becomes more aware of what is going on around him, hence he has greater mastery of the vehicle and greater driving safety'. Such specious pleading presumably sought to justify the fact that the Athon had no weather protection of any sort . . .

Buying Hints

1. The belt-driven single-cam engines (P200/P250) suffer from belt stretch and from tensioner problems. Evidence of a recent belt change is thus a good sign.

2. All Lamborghini V8s are prone to small-end wear: listen for a clicking sound on tickover. Oil leaks are another known problem.

3. Steering wobble is a sign that the struts are worn; replacement can be expensive.

4. The rear swivels need to be greased every 1,000km or 600 miles but rarely are; the result is wheel wobble. Check for this by jacking up the rear of the car and waggling each wheel side to side. Don't confuse this type of play with that from worn wheel bearings – some slight bearing play is common, as the bearings are not of the taper variety.

5. Check the water hoses running underneath the car: the hoses should be in good condition and the metal elements uncorroded.

6. The Urraco in particular was made in an era of miserable rust-resistance as far as Italian cars were concerned. Try to buy a non-UK car from a dry climate.

7. These hints apply equally to the Silhouette and Jalpa; for the latter there is still reasonable parts availability, and the cars are less rust-prone.

The interior of the Urraco features two somewhat symbolic and very upright rear seats, their headrests conspiring further to reduce rear visibility. (LAT)

The Countach

The chiselled looks of the Countach are at their purest – and their most futuristic? – in the LP400. Here a British-owned example poses with its flat-12 rival, the Ferrari Berlinetta Boxer. (LAT)

How do you replace a car as breathtaking – as charismatic – as the Miura? Playing it safe clearly wasn't an option, because in 1971 Bertone and Lamborghini collaborated on the most extraordinary supercar the world has ever seen. The Countach didn't merely shift the goalposts: it reconfigured the entire playing-field. Never – McLaren F1 included – has there been a more extreme road car.

Unveiled on the Bertone stand at the 1971 Geneva motor show, the prototype Countach was a futuristic yellow mid-engined ultra-wedge with stunning scissor-action upward swinging doors, and was the work of studio head Marcello Gandini. Under this showcar exterior was an all-new structure of square tubing clad with welded-on steel panels; this was sometimes described as a monocoque, but semi-monocoque would be more precise. There was also an all-new mechanical layout, with the engine now mounted fore and aft, the gearbox ahead of it between the seats and controlled by a short central lever. Step-down gears drove a shaft that ran beside the sump to the final drive.

It appears that the reason for the

Countach LP400
1974–78

ENGINE:
60-degree V12, mid-mounted longitudinally; aluminium-alloy construction

Capacity	3929cc
Bore x stroke	82mm x 62mm
Valve actuation	Twin overhead camshafts per bank of cylinders, chain-driven
Compression ratio	10.5:1
Carburettors	Six Weber horizontal twin-choke 45DC0E23
Power	375bhp (DIN) at 8000rpm
Torque	266lb ft at 5000rpm

TRANSMISSION:
Rear-wheel drive; five-speed Lamborghini-made gearbox with synchromesh on all ratios including reverse; ZF limited-slip differential Final drive 4.08:1

SUSPENSION:
Front: Independent by unequal-length double wishbones, coil springs, Koni telescopic dampers; anti-roll bar
Rear: Independent by unequal-length double wishbones, coil springs, twin Koni telescopic dampers each side; anti-roll bar

STEERING:
Rack-and-pinion; no power assistance; 3.2 turns lock to lock

BRAKES:
Front: 10.5-in (265mm) Girling ventilated disc
Rear: 10.5-in (265mm) Girling ventilated disc Girling vacuum servo, dual circuit

WHEELS/TYRES:
Campagnolo cast magnesium-alloy 14in wheels; five-stud; 7.5in front rims and 9.5in rear rims Tyres 205/70VR14 front and 215/70VR14 rear, Michelin XWX

BODYWORK:
Two-seater, two-door aluminium-alloy coupé designed by Bertone and built by Lamborghini

DIMENSIONS:

Length	15ft 7in (4.14m)
Wheelbase	8ft 0.5in (2.45m)
Track, front	4ft 11.1in (1.50m)
Track, rear	4ft 11.8in (1.52m)
Width	6ft 2.4in (1.99m)
Height	3ft 6.1in (1.07m)

WEIGHT (KERB):
27.0cwt (1,370kg)

PERFORMANCE:
(Source: *Road & Track*)

Max speed	192mph (309kph) est.

(the highest maximum speeds achieved by magazine testers are 175mph and 185mph)

0-60mph	6.8sec
0-100mph	13.3sec

NUMBER MADE:
150

PRICE (INCLUDING TAXES) WHEN NEW:
£18,000 (1975)

Countach LP400S
1978–82

As LP400 except:
ENGINE:

Carburettors	Six Weber horizontal twin-choke 40DCOE
Power	353bhp at 7500rpm
Torque	260lb ft at 5500rpm

TRANSMISSION:
ZF limited slip differential. Final drive 4.09:1

WHEELS/TYRES:
Campagnolo cast magnesium-alloy 15in wheels, five-stud, 8.5in front rims and 12in rear rims Tyres 205/50VR front and 345/35VR rear, Pirelli P7

DIMENSIONS:

Track, front	4ft 10.7in (1.49m)
Track, rear	5ft 4.3in (1.635m)

WEIGHT (KERB):
28.3cwt (1,438kg)

PERFORMANCE:
(Source: *Road & Track*)

Max speed	164mph estimated
0-60mph	5.9sec
0-100mph	14.4sec

NUMBER MADE:
237

PRICE (INCLUDING TAXES) WHEN NEW:
£45,000 (1982)

Countach LP500S
1982–85

As LP400S except:
ENGINE:

Capacity	4754cc
Bore x stroke	85.5mm x 69.0mm
Compression ratio	9.2:1
Fuel system	Six Weber horizontal twin-choke 45DCOE carburettors Bosch K-Jetronic injection (US)
Power	375bhp (DIN) at 7000rpm
Torque	302lb ft at 4500rpm

BRAKES:
Front: 11.8in (300mm) Girling ventilated disc
Rear: 11.1in (280mm) Girling ventilated disc

Girling vacuum-servo, dual circuit

DIMENSIONS:

Track, rear	5ft 3.2in (1.605m)
Width	6ft 8.7in (2.00m)

WEIGHT (KERB):
26.0cwt (1,321kg)

PERFORMANCE:
(Source: *Autocar*)

Max speed	164mph
0-60mph	5.6sec
0-100mph	12.9sec
30-50mph in top	9.8sec
50-70mph in top	7.4sec

NUMBER MADE:
321

PRICE (INCLUDING TAXES) WHEN NEW:
£49,885 (rear wing £1,144.25 extra), 1982

Countach Quattrovalvole
1985–90

As LP500S except:
ENGINE:

Capacity	5167cc
Bore x stroke	85.5mm x 75mm
Valve actuation	Four valves per cylinder
Compression ratio	9.5:1
Carburettors	Six Weber twin-choke horizontal 44DCNF
Power	455bhp (SAE) at 7000rpm
Torque	340lb ft at 5200rpm

WHEELS/TYRES
Tyres 225/50VR front and 345/35VR rear, Pirelli P7

DIMENSIONS:

Track, front	5ft 0.6in (1.54m);
Track, rear	5ft 3.4in (1.61m)

WEIGHT (KERB):
29.3cwt (1,487kg)

PERFORMANCE
(Source: *Autocar*)

Max speed	178mph
0-60mph	5.1sec
0-100mph	11.0sec
30-50mph in top	Not available
50-70mph in top	Not available

NUMBER MADE:
618

PRICE (INCLUDING TAXES) WHEN NEW:
£65,900 (1985)

At the Geneva show in March 1971 Bertone unleashed the prototype Countach on a startled public and press. At the time few believed that it was a proposed production car, assuming it to be purely a 'show special'. The most obvious difference from the production car is the rear end treatment. (LAT)

Below: Another view of the early Countach, showing the door-opening arrangement. Although it makes it easier to get out of the car in a confined space, because the door cuts into the roof the interior is likely to get soaked on a wet day. Lamborghini never resolved the rather inconvenient split side windows. (LAT)

abandonment of the Miura's transverse engine was Ferruccio Lamborghini's conviction that there should be more than the odd glass panel separating the occupants from the engine; it was, in his view, more practical to insulate human frailty from mechanical complexity with a longitudinally mounted engine. That is as it may be; another benefit of the layout was that it increased forward weight distribution, thereby helping to

tackle the *in extremis* oversteer and high-speed front-end lift to which the Miura was prone.

Immediately after the return of the Countach from Geneva, extensive development testing started, and a more definitive version of the car appeared at the Paris show in October 1971. At this time Lamborghini was cash-strapped and the money was simply lacking to develop a reliable production version of the 4,971cc V12

used in the prototype. Furthermore, with both Countach and Urraco under development, the research and development department was heavily overloaded, and the launch of both cars took place far later than intended. This caused sales to be lost, and contributed to the downfall of the company.

Against this background, Bob Wallace put on a high mileage driving the car up and down the roads

between Sant'Agata and Florence, which formed part of the Mugello circuit and included the Futa and Raticosa passes. Lamborghini also tested extensively at the Modena *Aeroautodromo* and at the Varano de' Melegari circuit near Parma. Both Lamborghini plant manager Paolo Stanzani and engineer Massimo Parenti went along for much of the testing, conducting wool-tuft airflow tests and taking notes from a Telemax

thermo-couple 'black box'.

The decision to put the Countach into production was made in May 1972. Wallace and Stanzani took the prototype to Sicily for the Targa Florio and after a fast and troublefree return trip, co-owners of the company Ferruccio Lamborghini and Georges-Henri Rossetti gave the go-ahead. Stanzani set the goals that the company was trying to achieve: the Countach was to be a *macchini sportive*

No spoilers, no wheelarch flares: the LP400 is quite a contrast with the LP400S that followed. (LAT)

The LP400 on the road – and in perspective

If you are at all used to driving high-performance cars of the late 1960s and the early 1970s the Countach comes as something of a shock. It is not much bigger than a Miura, but *seems* to be a much bigger car. It is a car full of angles and by today's standards has very poor ergonomics. The doors, supported on hydraulic struts, open up to reveal narrow seats below the enormous sills.

When you have manoeuvred yourself into the driving seat, you find that forward vision is poor because the Countach is only 3ft 6in high, while to look sideways you have to peer over the door frames which come up to eye level. Unsurprisingly, rear vision through the mirror is severely restricted, and many owners have relied on a mirror stuck on the windscreen to give marginally better vision.

There are few chances to drive a Countach flat out and there are few drivers able to exploit its handling envelope. Remember, also, that handling of the Countach varies from example to example, depending how and how well the suspension is set up and on the condition of the dampers and springs.

While it is obviously a matter of opinion and a lot depends on the condition of the examples that one has had the good fortune (or misfortune to drive) I consider that a

Miura has a better gearchange and better handling than a Countach. Only too often there is a jerky throttle on a Countach because of poor maintenance, the clutch is heavier than that of the Miura, the gearchange is stiffer and because it is alongside the driver (and not ahead of him, as is usual) changing gear is that much more awkward.

From the moment that you fire up the engine, your ears are assailed by a whooping wail of exhaust noise and as you accelerate the bellowing and whooping rises in a crescendo, accompanied by carburettor induction roar. Few will have ever driven such a free-revving engine, but nothing much happens up to 4,000rpm and then the engine speedily screams its way up to 8,000rpm. One of the important aspects of Lamborghini engine development was the extension of the safe rev range.

By any standard the Countach has superlative handling, even when it is not as well set up as it should be. Adhesion is very high indeed but, like all high-powered mid-engined cars until very recently, when the back end breaks away in the dry the prospects of a run-of the-mill driver getting it all back under control again are marginal. Despite those enormous Pirellis, a Countach will break away very easily in the wet, but in these circumstances you can usually get it

all back again. Because of the absence of power assistance, the steering is relatively low-geared, especially at low manoeuvring speeds, and it is not too difficult to let the Countach get away from you momentarily in these circumstances.

There are few places or opportunities for approaching the sort of speed of which a Countach is capable. Even if you do find an apparently near-empty autobahn or autostrada, at even 150mph you will be covering a mile in 24 seconds, closing on traffic ahead at a phenomenal rate, and the Countach may well be jumping all over what you thought was a smooth road.

A Countach may accelerate from 0–60mph in a shade under 7 seconds, but what really counts with a high-speed car on modern roads is just how quickly and safely you can overtake. In reasonable fettle an original LP400 will travel from 60mph to 80mph in about 6.5 seconds in second gear and from 80mph to 100mph in about the same time. This is sensible, safe performance in the hands of a relatively competent driver.

By no means is a Countach every enthusiast's choice of classic car and by itself being an enthusiast does not make you any better a driver or capable of handling such a powerful car. A Countach is a car for very able, experienced drivers.

What's in a name?

Designated at the factory as the Tipo 112, after its chassis project number, the public designation of the prototype Countach was LP500 (*Longitudinal Posteriore Cinque Litri* or 'Longitudinal rear-engine 5-litre'). The name 'Countach' is said to derive

from a Piedmontese expletive, most politely translated as 'Cor!' But there often appears to be a touch of the imaginative when it comes to telling stories about Lamborghini names. According to some sources, the word was 'plucked out of the air' when a

name was needed for the first showing of the car at Geneva. Another version is that a Bertone employee, seeing the design for the first time, uttered *Countach!* in appreciative amazement. One can understand why.

The interior scarcely changed over the years. On the LP400 the dials are from Stewart-Warner. (LAT)

The Campagnolo wheels are unfussy, and in character with the car. (LAT)

stradale, and the ultimate of that breed of high-performance road cars not intended for competition. It had to combine the highest possible performance, coupled with stability, manoeuvrability, and a high level of comfort for driver and passenger.

It was also decided that price was secondary and that the new car would be sold only to selected customers, people already known to the company. This was because Miuras had fallen into the wrong hands – poor drivers who crashed them, and owners with an unsavoury reputation. As times became harder and cars more difficult to sell, this goal was abandoned and Lamborghini became thankful for any sale that could be made.

The first production prototype appeared at the Geneva show in March 1973 and the final version, with minor changes, was exhibited at Paris later that year. Production did not get under way, however, until 1974. One of the most important changes from the prototype was to revert to the original 3,929cc engine; with six horizontal Weber 45DCOE23 twin-choke carburettors, this developed 375bhp at 8,000rpm. Ignition was looked after

by two Marelli distributors.

For cooling Lamborghini used a pressurised set-up with two copper radiators, one each side of the engine, with a cross-over connecting system, and these were mounted just to the rear of the fuel tank. As on the prototype, the engine was installed longitudinally with the gearbox ahead of the engine, which meant a short gear linkage and a direct and positive change. Another advantage of this layout was that it provided good access to the alternator, distributors, timing chain and water pumps. Throughout the car there was extensive use of magnesium-alloy, including for the cam covers, sump, engine mounts, and oil-pump and oil-filter housings.

The Fitchel & Sachs clutch, which was similar to that used on the Porsche 917 sports-racer, was mounted on the end of the crankshaft in a vast magnesium-alloy casing and there was a five-speed indirect-drive gearbox, also with a magnesium-alloy casing. From the secondary shaft of the gearbox the drive was transmitted by a transfer gear to a driveshaft. This driveshaft ran in two bearings and

passed through the engine sump to the ZF limited-slip differential immediately behind the engine.

Stanzani developed a round-tube chassis frame for the production car with the aim of combining low weight and rigidity. A roll-cage structure surrounded the cockpit to provide maximum safety in the event of an accident and a box-steel section that

Page 92 top: A side view does not show the Countach at its best – despite the NACA ducts ahead of the rear wheels, the car has a rather slab-sided appearance. It looks so much better from other angles. Page 92 bottom: A plain unadorned LP400. From this angle the box-like air intakes dominate the upper surfaces. Page 93 top: The main external difference between the LP400S of 1978 and the earlier cars is the former's chunky wheelarch extensions, needed to enclose the new and very wide low-profile Pirelli P7 tyres. This car was photographed at Monaco in 1981. Page 93 bottom: The 5-litre LP500S Countach appeared in 1982 and gave an immediate boost to flagging sales. Even in its original two-valve form it is a much more relaxing car to drive than its predecessor. Here it again displays the so-called 'scissors' doors. (All LAT)

Car No 20: Driving an early Countach

On a visit to Lamborghini on behalf of Classic & Sports Car magazine, Mark Hughes was lucky enough to drive not only a Miura SV but also the 20th Countach off the lines, in the company of chief test driver Valentino Balboni. He was profoundly impressed . . .

Unusually – and rather flatteringly – finished in blue, this 1974 car is only the 20th Countach built. The driving impressions here relate to this car. (LAT)

Give the fuel pump a few seconds to prime the battery of carbs nestling above crackle-black cam covers and open the throttle slightly as you turn the key. The V12 cracks into life instantly, emitting a deep-chested beat and gently strumming at the car as it warms through.

The arrow-straight, wide-open, empty roads around Sant'Agata suit the Countach down to the ground. My first few full-throttle blasts reveal a blend of shattering pace yet easy tractability. The acceleration is relentless, with a strong, clean, seamless pull from 1,000rpm to 8,000rpm.

I'm concerned about exploring the last 1,500rpm, but Valentino seems not to mind. Added intensity is discernible from 4,500rpm, just at the point where the V12's rumble sharpens into a howl, but this engine is outstanding for its range.

A top speed of 170 is credible . . . More relevant is the effortlessness with which the Countach strides towards the horizon. Superb aerodynamics and long-legged 26mph per 1,000rpm gearing in top make a seriously brisk gallop feel like a trot.

The car slices through the air with rare efficiency, a judgement that's confirmed by lifting off at speed and feeling how well the car sustains its momentum. You can also feel downforce acting to keep the car tied to the road . . .

. . . poor visibility is a distinct drawback in traffic, at junctions, and on street corners. The view behind is adequate, but three-quarter vision is non-existent without exterior mirrors and you can't avoid taking slip roads on a wing and a prayer. Manoeuvring is just as awkward. When you need to turn the car round, you size up your reversing line while you can still see it, as you would in a van. All the same, you end up edging back more or less blindly.

Enough of the impracticalities. With the mass so low and centred, handling is unimpeachable. This car is so uncompromisingly developed that it rewards its driver handsomely when conditions are right.

A twisty road reveals uncannily faithful responses to steering and throttle. Driven with precision, the Countach does all – and more – you could wish of it, simply heading where it's directed. The only limiting factor results from the invisibility of the nose from the driving seat preventing total accuracy through corners.

Only in one area does the Countach fail to exceed the Miura SV's formidable standards. The Countach has an edge in precision, balance and predictability, but its grip on relatively skinny tall-shouldered Michelin XWXs (the original specification) can be defeated, although squirming side-walls and a mild progression towards oversteer give plenty of warning.

Nothing else can be faulted. The brakes are powerful and progressive, the steering taut and communicative, the gearchange crisp and fast. All the controls are pleasant to use, decently weighted but not too heavy . . .

Perhaps the final verdict on the Countach's success as the ultimate in supercar individualism is how it gets noticed. On the streets of Sant'Agata crowds gather to admire this little projectile sparkling in the sunlight. Some people with long memories know what it is, but others, taken in by the other-worldly looks, genuinely take it for a new model from the factory down the road. The Countach was that far ahead of its time.

was ahead of, above, and to the rear of the cockpit supported the roof. In addition there were two roll-bars behind the seats.

Hung on this frame was new competition-type Rose-jointed suspension, incorporating magnesium-alloy hub carriers front and rear. At the front the coil-spring suspension was by unequal-length wishbones, combined spring/damper units and an anti-roll bar mounted behind the suspension. Lamborghini used a more complicated system at the rear, with single upper transverse links, lower wishbones, and two forward-facing radius arms. In addition there was an anti-roll bar and twin spring/damper units per wheel. These dampers were lightweight Konis with aluminium-alloy bodies and were fully adjustable for bump and rebound. It was consequently very important with a Countach (as it had been with the Miura) to ensure that the suspension was properly set up and kept that way.

Front and rear, Lamborghini specified Girling four-piston brakes with ventilated alloy callipers. Steering was rack-and-pinion in a magnesium-alloy housing, but there was still no power assistance and nor would there be on any Countach.

Although the prototype had a steel body, Bertone used aluminium-alloy panelling for the production bodies, riveted to the tubular frame. As the panels had a thickness of only 1mm, they were very vulnerable to damage in minor accidents or simply as a result of people leaning on them. The spare wheel was housed in the nose, leaving no room for luggage, but there was a small boot in the tail behind the engine.

The original prototype featured electronic digital instruments and a pioneering fault-display instrument that showed a diagram of the chassis and lit up to show any component that was not functioning correctly. For the production car a conventional and much less dramatic dashboard

arrangement was used.

One of the less attractive features of the Countach was the use of horizontally-split side windows, meaning that only part of the window could be opened. This restricted entry of fresh air into the cockpit, which became rather stuffy – even if the car was fitted with air-conditioning. Still, that was the price to be paid for the Countach's dramatic looks – and the original LP400 is surely the best looking of all Countach models, its body uncluttered by the aerodynamic devices of later models, its tail shapely and neat. As for that age-old 'wottle-it-do-mister?' question, throughout the history of the Countach there have been sundry claims and counter-claims about maximum speed. Over the years the weight of the Countach rose steadily and power output

The rather cramped interior of this LP500S is much the same as on earlier cars. Efforts had, however, been made to improve the quality of the trim and general finish. (LAT)

Lamborghini and the BMW M1

BMW racing director Jochen Neerpasch conceived the M1 in 1976, and it was intended to be the first car to be built in quantity by the BMW Motorsport division. The M1 was planned as a limited-edition supercar that could also be used for competition work.

Originally, the M1 was to have had a 3-litre V10 engine and it was intended to race it in Group 5 'Silhouette' events that required a minimum production of 400 cars. The M1 eventually emerged as a mid-engined coupé with a 3.5-litre six-cylinder engine developing 277bhp at 6,500rpm, a five-speed ZF transaxle, a tubular steel chassis, and a glassfibre body styled by Giugiaro of Italdesign.

BMW decided that the project was too big to be undertaken by the Motorsport division and too small for production at Munich, so manufacture was sub-contracted to Lamborghini. To enable it to undertake what was a major project, Lamborghini obtained a grant from the Italian government equivalent to more than £1 million. The Lamborghini management decided that there were better ways of spending the money, and expended most of it on the Cheetah off-road project. Lamborghini did however complete four M1 prototypes during

1977 and carried out development testing. BMW was unhappy with the standards of workmanship at Saint'Agata and it became obvious that Lamborghini was in financial difficulties; when a receiver was appointed, BMW cancelled the contract.

Giugiaro rescued the project for BMW by reorganising production. Marchesi of Modena constructed the chassis, Trasformazioni Italiana Resina moulded the bodies, Italdesign assembled the M1s, and Baur in Stuttgart installed the drivetrain – with BMW carrying out final checks and rectification at Munich. BMW abandoned the idea of running the cars in the Group 5 'Silhouette' class and, instead, the M1s competed during 1979–80 in the Procar series organised by Jochen Neerpasch as supporting races to Grands Prix. In all 455 of these 160mph-plus cars were made. Lamborghini had lost a golden opportunity.

Lamborghini's failure to accord adequate attention to the BMW M1 project was a tragic waste of the company's potential. Here a prototype is on test in Italy. (LAT/Stefanini)

became fettered by emission controls. Claiming to be the fastest production car in the world is a good marketing weapon, but it means very little in terms of everyday motoring. The reality is that a Countach in good engine tune should be capable of achieving 170mph without leaving a trail of oil smoke behind it. Some claim as high as 185mph and the reputable American magazine *Road & Track* estimated a maximum speed of 192mph. This was based on the argument that if the car would attain 7,000rpm in top and keep pulling

strongly, then the test team did not question its ability to attain 8,000rpm and thus top out at 192mph. Many commentators – and the author – regard this conclusion as optimistic and fallacious.

This was in 1976, with an LP400, and within two years this model had been replaced: after three years away, Dallara returned to Lamborghini to update the Countach, working on a consultancy basis, and with his changes it became the LP400S in 1978. Dallara based his modifications around the ultra-low-profile Pirelli P7

tyres then newly available and thus his changes were in the main to the suspension geometry. In addition there were moulded glassfibre wheelarch fairings to accommodate these tyres and the 8in-wide front and 12in-wide rear wheels.

At the front there was a small spoiler under the nose, while inside the seats were raised slightly, as was the tunnel in the roof, there originally because of the periscope rear mirror on prototype cars. That was about it for the changes, but in 1979 it was decided to reduce the power a little to

The 5-litre two-valve engine of the LP500. Bizzarrini's original design was brilliant and the same basic engine powers today's Murciélago. Lamborghini V12 engines are always a delight to behold. (LAT)

make the Countach more drivable; fitted with smaller-choke 40DCOE carburettors the V12 engine developed 353bhp in this revised format.

Lamborghini's continuing fraught financial situation necessitated the Countach remaining in production for far longer than the company might have wished. Continuing development, however, ensured that it remained at the forefront of the supercar performance league – while very real efforts were made to ensure that later versions were more practical. No supercar is ever going to be

completely practical, but Lamborghini's engineers had gone a long way to achieving that goal by the time the Countach was ready to be replaced by the Diablo.

Following the acquisition of the company by the Mimrams, work started on an improved version of the Countach. Engineer Luigi Marmaroli joined the company to work on the revised car and on other special projects, under the direction of Giulio Alfieri, and at the March 1982 Geneva motor show the revised LP500S appeared, with a 4,754cc engine. This

boasted redesigned combustion chambers, a lower compression ratio, and larger carburettors, along with Marelli electronic ignition; power steering remained unavailable.

The external appearance was substantially unchanged, apart from a dramatic – and expensive – cambered rear wing offered as an optional extra. It seems that the only effect this appendage had was to cut back the potential maximum speed, claimed by Lamborghini as 186mph – although no magazine tested the car in conditions whereby anything closely approaching

The Countach in Endurance Racing

In 1985 Danielle Audetto, one-time works Lancia rally driver and former Ferrari team manager, joined Lamborghini as director of public relations and sports director. Neither the Mimrams nor Emile Novaro, (a long-standing associate of the Mimrams, who appointed him managing director) were opposed to running the Countach in competition, provided that the prospects of success were good and the cost was not excessive. They probably allowed themselves to be carried away by the enthusiasm of Portman Garages, the British concessionaires, for in reality there was no serious prospect of success.

It was considered that in developed form and properly prepared the Countach QV could do well in endurance racing and the original aim was a good result at Le Mans. Engineer Luigi Marmaroli had developed a 5.7-litre version of the four-valve engine and this was dispatched to Spice Engineering at Silverstone for them to build a suitable car. What emerged, resplendent in black paint, was a car known as the Countach QVX. It was a near-enough standard Tiga GC285. Sponsorship came primarily from Unipart. It needs to be emphasised that the QVX was a Lamborghini Countach in name only.

Portman Garages was responsible for the costs of building the chassis and organising the team. Lamborghini, and in particular Marmaroli, was responsible for engineering development and the factory was to supply race engineers. After completion the new car was tested at Silverstone and later in the year at Monza, during which latter exercise driver Mauro Baldi turned in some very encouraging times. An entry was made in the last race of the 1986 season, the non-Championship Southern Seas 500 held at Kyalami in South Africa on 22 November.

At Kyalami the driver of the black 'Lamborghini' was Tiff Needell and the opposition, as was usual in these races, came from Porsche 962s and 956Bs, which made up the bulk of the field in this category of racing. It was a minor race and works teams were conspicuous by their absence. The race was run in two heats, totalling 219.30 miles (352.85km). After finishing seventh in the first heat, Needell finished fifth on aggregate behind a quartet of Porsche entries. As Porsche writer Michael Cotton commented, 'it sounded lovely'.

During 1986 the project had been underfunded, testing had proved largely inconclusive, and the performance at Kyalami had not been particularly encouraging. The Mimrams realised, in effect, that they had made a mistake in supporting the project and it was abandoned. The prospects of competing successfully had not been properly thought through, for if the car had raced in 1986–87 Group C Championship events it would have been competing against powerful and well-financed Porsche teams, as well as the works Jaguars and the Saubers, which were heavily backed by Mercedes-Benz.

Kyalami, 1986, and Tiff Needell in the QVX is behind a Zakspeed; he finished fifth on aggregate, with four Porsches ahead of him. (LAT)

this speed could be obtained.

At long last, in 1984, Lamborghini gladdened the hearts of wealthy enthusiasts in the United States by having the Countach certified for the US market – albeit at one remove, via an independent importer. For compliance with Stateside regulations the cars traded their Webers for a Bosch K-Jetronic fuel-injection system. An ex-works 'Federal' Countach only arrived – as an injected QV – in 1986.

Back in Europe, in 1982 *Autocar* magazine road-tested an LP500S, collected directly from the factory. The test was published in the issue of 9 October and the testers' comments make interesting reading:

'On arrival, we were somewhat horrified to learn that the only 500S available was a nearly brand-new one, with only 239 kilometres (149 miles) on its mileometer. It was explained that whilst a Countach with 3,000 miles behind it would certainly be up to 500rpm faster in top speed, the considerable amount of engine bench

Left: The LP500S on the road. The rear view of the Countach is one of its most stylish aspects and these cars look particularly dramatic in white. (LAT)

Below: This photograph of the Countach production line at Sant'Agata was taken in October 1982 and although the factory was working well under capacity, sales were picking up, partly because of an improved economic climate. (LAT)

Paolo Stanzani and the Cizeta

Young engineer Paolo Stanzani, another ex-Ferrari man, joined Lamborghini at much the same time as Dallara and acted as both his assistant and as production manager. After Dallara left the company, he became technical director. Working with Bertone, he was largely responsible for the design and engineering development of the Urraco and for much of the development of the Countach. He left the company in 1975, having concluded that *de facto* managing director René Leimer was making too heavy demands on the development department.

In the 1980s Stanzani and other former Lamborghini staff joined a new project that seemed to have prospects of challenging Lamborghini in the supercar field and had the appearance of an updated Countach. The car was the Cizeta-Moroder V16T

backed by Claudio Zampolli, who had been assistant to Bob Wallace at Lamborghini. The somewhat extreme styling was the work of Marcello Gandini, and his involvement with the Cizeta nearly cost him his commission to work on the Diablo.

The Cizeta had a transversely-mounted 6-litre 64-valve V16 engine at the rear. A duplex chain in the centre of the block drove the eight overhead camshafts and there was a Bosch K-Jetronic fuel injection system. This power unit was claimed to develop 560bhp at 8,000rpm. There was a five-speed manual gearbox. Gandini's design made the Cizeta look like a longer, wider and smoother Countach. Certainly with an extra 10in of length and 4in of width it was much roomier inside than a Countach, and had much bigger doors.

Although journalists were able to

In later years Stanzani was involved with other former Lamborghini employees with the Cizeta, a car that looked like an updated Countach but had a V16 engine. Fortunately for Lamborghini, but unhappily for the Cizeta backers, the venture folded after only seven cars had been built.

drive it briefly, the Cizeta was never subjected to a full road test; Zampolli estimated a maximum speed of 204mph and 0-60mph in 4.5 seconds. After the prototype had been fully developed and tested, production started and six cars were built before the project folded. It was a great relief to Sant'Agata that this rather superior Lamborghini lookalike proved too massive an undertaking for its backers.

Gandini incorporated certain features of the Cizeta in the Diablo, notably the shape of the side windows.

running before installation ensured that the unit was at any rate initially run-in.

'Each V12 has six hours of being driven by an electric motor as its first breaking-in treatment. It is then started up and worked against a brake at various constant rpm between 2,000 and 6,000 in 1,000rpm intervals, at 1½ to 2 hours for each speed, after which its maximum power and torque are measured to ensure that the engine is up to specification.

'Lamborghini are by no means a big company, especially now in their leaned-down but apparently more efficient size, yet they have four fully equipped engine test houses in which this power unit preparation – two days of it – takes place.

'Certainly, the test car's engine didn't sound or feel tight or in the least bit unwilling. In typically warm Italian summer weather, it starts easily after a prod or two of accelerator pumps and will trickle without temperament or too much noise through built-up areas. But this is not a town car; it is for the open road, preferably clear of obstructions to the Countach's passage or forward vision.

The Countach Evoluzione

This was a one-off experimental car built by the factory in 1987. At heart it was a Quattrovalvole, but it had a carbonfibre central structure with reinforced honeycomb panelling. Although the engine was to the same specification as the 500QV, including carburation, ignition and compression ratio, the maker's power output figure was 490bhp at 7,000rpm. Make of that what you will, but what I make of it is that the power output was in fact the same as that of the QV. The *Evoluzione* was in reality a rolling test-bed to investigate various technologies, in particular the use of carbon-composites, and lessons learned from this prototype were profitably incorporated in the Diablo.

'The engine, without being too noisy, is always entirely dominant in sound, and so dominant in performance. You don't call up on it to do anything important at below 10mph in second, 30 in third, or 40 in the two uppermost gears; it is not enthusiastic about crankshaft speeds of less than 1,700rpm …'

Of especial interest are the comments about the engine bench tests before the power unit was installed in the car. Overall the Mimrams did much to raise standards to ensure that the buyer received a car of the quality that he expected. This, coupled with the overall enthusiasm of the new owners, did much to improve the morale of the workforce and many compared the *esprit de corps* with the heady, exciting days when Ferruccio Lamborghini ran the company.

As will be seen from the table on page 87, the *Autocar* testers achieved a mean maximum of 164mph, together with a best one-way speed of 165mph

The main distinguishing point of the LP500S is its optional rear spoiler, just visible in this shot. (LAT)

In 1985 Lamborghini introduced the Countach LP500S Quattrovalvole with a four-valve version of the 5,167cc V12 engine. Maximum speed of the 500QV is in excess of 180mph.

in conditions of almost no wind. Despite a new engine, the magazine's testers thus recorded, as far as can be traced, the best performance documented by any English-language magazine. It was also exactly the same maximum as the magazine had achieved in 1978 with the Countach's principal rival, the Ferrari BB512 – despite Ferrari claiming a maximum speed of 188mph. Clearly in the Lamborghini-versus-Ferrari supercar maximum-speed grudge match there was not much in it at the end of the day, one way or the other.

In terms of handling, steering and braking, there were no perceptible

differences between the new 5-litre car and its predecessor, although with the latest wide tyres, grip and traction were now truly exceptional. It accordingly remained a phenomenally safe car in skilled and experienced hands, but completely lethal in the hands of a less than truly able driver.

Where the LP500S scored was that it was generally much more refined, and was built and finished to higher standards than its predecessors. A further bonus was that Lamborghini had made a serious and sensible attempt at achieving a good cockpit layout, all the main dials now being clearly visible and the switches on the central console properly marked. Finally, for those for whom such things mattered, while earlier cars could average as little as 10-12mpg, the 5-litre's overall fuel consumption worked out at about 15mpg.

When the development of the LP500S had been completed, Alfieri and Marmaroli turned their attention to a four-valve-per-cylinder version of the Countach. This appeared in 1985 and had the engine capacity further increased to 5,167cc, resulting in an output of 455bhp at 7,000rpm – or a claimed 449bhp in 'federalised' US form. Of this the American magazine *Car and Driver* commented '. . . we doubt very much that all 449 horses were present. Our computations point to something like 370.' Other than the engine, there were few changes, apart from a taller engine cover, wider front tyres, and some minor suspension alterations.

The four-valver was certainly no faster in top speed than the original 5-litre and beyond the fact that four-valve-per-cylinder engines were then newly fashionable, it is difficult to see

This 1988 Quattrovalvole has been fitted with 'Anniversary' straked sill panels. Even today, the scissor-action doors are a surefire attention-getter. (LAT)

From the rear the taller engine-cover introduced on the QV is readily apparent. (LAT)

Above: A view of the 48-valve engine of the Countach LP500S Quattrovalvole. (LAT)

Right: White leather was a common choice by the time of the QV; note the pockets in the sill box-sections. (LAT)

Opposite above: On the road in the very last 'Anniversary' Countach. (LAT)

Opposite below: With the slatted air intakes and exits, the flanks of the 'Anniversary' have a very different look. (LAT)

what was achieved by that substantial increase in power, apart from slightly better acceleration and the elimination of a flat spot at around 3,500rpm.

In June 1985 *Road & Track* published driving impressions by Hans-Jürgen Tücherer, translated and adapted from the German by respected journalist Ron Wakefield. They make informative and amusing reading.

'Our test car was without the optional rear wing: too bad, for the wing certainly enhances the Lambo's aggressive look. But you don't buy a car for its looks alone – and this $80,000 (in Europe) car still has plenty of the weaknesses that are pretty much typical of many Italian exotics. Workmanship could be a lot better, for instance. On our car the shift gate wobbled and the accordion cover on the steering column fit[ted] poorly.

'Design faults are there too: The narrow, rather uncomfortable seats still can't be adjusted fully, making things more difficult than necessary for drivers more than 5ft 10in tall.

Fresh air remains available only through the air conditioning, because the windows can't be opened more than a hand's width – and (here Lamborghini shows a fine sense of austerity) not electrically, but by hand cranks! Also unchanged: bad reflections on the instrument glass, which obliterate any information in strong sunlight.

'It's open to question whether a 180mph car that gets fewer than 10mpg makes any sense these days. There just aren't any logical arguments

Buying Hints

1. As total production of the Countach amounted to close on 2,000 cars over a 16-year period, examples are not difficult to find, especially of the later Quattrovalvole cars built for six years and which amount to just under one-third of production. Pretty well all spare parts are available for these, and cars with full history, including a service record, can still be found.

2. Obtain the advice of an expert. A reputable Countach specialist may well know a car for sale elsewhere, and may have worked on it recently. In such circumstances an independent inspection might not even be necessary.

3. Look for a car that has already had a great deal of money spent on it. Buying a cheap Countach could be a ruinous experience.

4. All body parts for the Countach are available from the factory, and specialist Carrera Sport makes a lot of parts itself – in particular front spoilers and rear wings.

5. The rear edges of the front wings are wrapped around a steel former, and this acts as a trap for road dirt, so check here for corrosion. The alloy doors are built around a steel frame, and corrosion of the aluminium around the door edges is often a problem.

6. It is not unusual for a Countach to have been involved in an accident. Poorly fitting trim or ripply panels concealed with filler are obvious giveaways.

7. If tubes in the chassis have been replaced, check for the quality of welding.

8. Dampers can usually be rebuilt, making the main suspension expense likely to be replacement of worn Rose joints: there are ten each side in the rear suspension alone. Rattles from the suspension are a tell-tale sign – although this could be from the joints for the anti-roll bars. Bangs and clatters over potholes could be either, or indeed wear in the anti-roll bar clamp brackets; neither is a serious issue (fortunately, given the cost of replacing four Rose joints per anti-roll bar), and in the case of the clamp brackets simple shimming-up with brass will effect a cure. Check, finally, that the suspension tie rods have not been bent by having been used as jacking or tie-down points.

9. Steering that is heavier on one lock than the other could be the result of an incorrectly set-up caster angle.

10. Poor brakes may be a result of seized callipers – but be warned that by today's standards some might find the Countach's brakes disappointing even if they are working correctly. Replacement brake discs are very rarely needed but again are not cheap.

11. Front stub axles can fracture; Carrera Sport offers strengthened items that are cheaper than the equivalent ex-factory. Rear hubs can crack if a rear wheel is kerbed; repair is feasible, or Carrera Sport can offer its own replacements.

12. The front-to-back oil pipes can become porous: oil drips or an oily right-hand sill are something of a giveaway.

13. A replacement exhaust in stainless steel is not horrifyingly expensive but a replacement clutch, lasting up to 55,000 miles, will not be cheap, any more than an overhauled gearbox. It is normal for second gear to baulk until the oil is warm.

14. The Marelli ignition module used from the 5000S onwards is vulnerable to damp. Difficult starting or cutting out suggest a problem. If a car still has a Marelli module, budget for its future replacement.

15. Don't be tempted by a car with a cracked windscreen: you could buy a respectable secondhand Fiesta with the money you'd need to replace the screen . . .

for buying such a machine; what reasonable human being would want a car that's so loud, uncomfortable and hard to get into? More conservative types would say that only crazies or neurotics need such merchandise.

'But, friends, let reasonable people ridicule and bitch; they merely haven't driven a Lamborghini Countach Quattrovalvole, haven't experienced the fascination for themselves. And it's that pleasure of driving that's the

only argument for a Countach – the only one that counts.'

The year 1988 marked the 25th anniversary of the founding of Lamborghini and as yet the Diablo was a long way from production. Hence the 'Anniversary', which was intended to boost sales. Mechanically, it was unchanged from the QV, but there were bodywork changes that made this model look distinctive. At the front there was a new carbonfibre bumper

and a redesigned front spoiler, and at the rear another carbonfibre bumper. On the sides of the front wings at the bottom there were double-strake inlets and in the same position ahead of the rear wheels were triple-strake ducts. The strakes were primarily intended to improve cooling of the brakes, just as new and much neater inlets to boost engine cooling replaced the big 'ears' so familiar on earlier Countach models.

Close-up of the new intakes on the 'Anniversary'. (LAT)

The front spoiler also incorporates straked vents. (LAT)

The interior of the 'Anniversary' is less of a black hole when upholstered in pale grey, as here. (LAT)

Horracio Pagani, who in recent years has built his own Pagani Zonda cars, was responsible for the styling changes. Some critics regard his cosmetic rework of the Countach body as 'absurd' or 'ridiculous', but it achieved what it was intended to do, which was to breathe new life into an old model. Overall, it was certainly a much neater car than its predecessors, and sales totalling 657 were more than enough to satisfy Chrysler. The last Countach was made in May 1990; total production in all its forms, ignoring prototypes, was 1,983 cars.

Having built such an advanced and successful car as the Miura, Lamborghini had admirably risen to the challenge of building an equally advanced successor. Overall, the Countach was a less practical car than the Miura, but it initiated a style that established the bloodline for future Lamborghinis. It also enjoyed a production life of over 15 years. Although this was to a considerable extent necessitated by Lamborghini's continuing financial problems, it was a remarkable achievement that a very expensive supercar could hold a prominent position in the marketplace for so long.

The Silhouette and Jalpa

Introduced in 1976, the Silhouette was an attempt by Bertone at building a Porsche-style Targa-top body. Performance was excellent, but because of poor sales the car was listed for only two years.

At the Geneva motor show in March 1976 the Targa-topped Silhouette was unveiled. A clever adaptation of the Urraco by Bertone, it transformed the look of the small Lamborghini and gave the company a more sporting two-seater model to combat the Ferrari 308GTB.

The Silhouette retained the basic Urraco fastback roofline, but with a reshaped rear incorporating sail panels, a strong rollbar to protect occupants, and a recessed vertical rear window. The detachable glassfibre roof stowed behind the front seats when not in use, in the space that in the Urraco was occupied by the occasional rear seats. Squared-off flared wheelarches completed the new look, and were very much in the Bertone house style during the Gandini years; they were filled by bigger and wider Campagnolo wheels described as being of 'five-cylinder' design and shod with the latest Pirelli P7 tyres.

Other changes included a very deep front spoiler, which incorporated an engine oil cooler and scoops to cool the front brakes, and a redesigned interior and instrument layout – not that either showed much improvement over the original.

Other than shorter recalibrated dampers, stiffer suspension, and thicker anti-roll bars, the running gear was basically unchanged, the 250bhp 3-litre quad-cam P300 engine being carried over from the Urraco.

Possibly hindered by a lack of US certification, the newcomer did not sell, and only 52 were made, over two years. It is thus difficult to find anyone who has even driven one, apart from Ron Wakefield, the European Editor of the American magazine *Road & Track*, who visited the works to drive the prototype. His comments about the Silhouette make interesting reading:

'Apart from being primed that this was a "harder" car, I expected a bone-jarring ride but was pleasantly surprised to find that this was not the case. The Silhouette is stiffer than the Urraco but still a long way from bone-jarring, and despite the missing roof section (*this had been stowed away*) the body is rigid enough to deal with poor road surfaces without undue flexing,' he wrote.

'The steering as you would expect with the fat tyres is fairly heavy. It has lost none of the precision of the Urraco, but rather gained some; too much, in fact, probably because of the tyres. There's even more of the go-kart effect (one senses every twist in the road surface in the steering wheel) and on choppy bumps the wheel gets too lively in the hands.

'As for hard cornering, I was left a bit confused by the Silhouette and would need to spend some time on a race track to sort it out completely. The Urraco on 250/70 tyres has lots of

Silhouette P300
1976–78

ENGINE:
90-degree V8 mid-mounted transversely; aluminium-alloy construction throughout

Capacity	2997cc
Bore x stroke	86mm x 64.5mm
Valve actuation	Twin overhead camshafts per bank of cylinders, chain driven
Compression ratio	10:1
Carburettors	Four twin-choke downdraught Weber 40 DCNF
Power	260bhp (DIN) at 7500rpm
Torque	203lb ft at 3500rpm

TRANSMISSION:
Rear-wheel drive; five-speed Lamborghini-made gearbox with synchromesh on all forward gears and reverse
Final drive 4.0:1

SUSPENSION:
Front: MacPherson struts, lower links; anti-roll bar
Rear: MacPherson struts, reversed lower wishbones; anti-roll bar

STEERING:
Rack-and-pinion; no power assistance; four turns lock-to-lock

BRAKES:
Front: Girling 10.9in (275mm) ventilated disc
Rear: Girling 10.9in (275mm) ventilated disc
Dual circuit; servo assistance

WHEELS/TYRES:
Campagnolo cast magnesium-alloy 15in wheels, five-stud fixing; 8in front and 11in rear rims
Tyres 195/50VR front and 285/40VR rear, Pirelli P7

BODYWORK:
Two-door, two-seat Targa-top steel body by Bertone with detachable glassfibre top

DIMENSIONS:

Length	14ft 4.2in (4.40m)
Track, front	4ft 10.3in (1.48m)
Track, rear	5ft 0.5in 1.525m)
Width	5ft 5in (1.65m)
Height	3ft 7.9in (1.115m)

WEIGHT (KERB):
24.6cwt (1,247kg)

PERFORMANCE:
(Source: *Road & Track*)

Max speed	147mph
0–60mph	6.8sec
0–100mph	16.1sec
30–50mph in top	Not available
50–70mph in top	Not available

PRICE INCLUDING TAX WHEN NEW:
No UK price quoted

NUMBER MADE:
52

Jalpa P350
1982–88

As Silhouette except:
ENGINE:

Capacity	3485cc
Bore x stroke	86.0mm x 75.0mm
Compression ratio	9.0:1
Carburettors	Four Weber twin-choke horizontal 42DCNF
Power	250bhp (DIN) at 7000rpm
Torque	235lb ft at 3250rpm

BRAKES:
Front: Girling 10in (255mm) ventilated discs
Rear: Girling 10in (255mm) ventilated discs
Servo-assisted, dual circuit

WHEELS/TYRES:
Cast-alloy 17in wheels; rims 7.5-inch front and rear
Tyres 205/55VR front and 225/50VR rear, Pirelli P7

DIMENSIONS:

Length	14ft 10in (4.215m)
Width	5ft 5.1in (1.655m)

WEIGHT (KERB):
29.5cwt (1499kg)

PERFORMANCE:
(Source: *Motor*)

Max speed	149.7mph (see text)
0–60mph	5.8sec
0–100mph	16.0sec
30–50mph in top	7.8sec
50–70mph in top	6.1sec

PRICE INCLUDING TAX WHEN NEW (1983):
£26,423

NUMBER MADE:
421 (some sources give alternative figures of 310 and 420 cars)

The Silhouette with its roof removed. The squared wheelarches transform the once-delicate lines of the former Urraco body.

cornering power and surely the Silhouette would deliver even more in a skidpan test. But despite fairly high tyre pressures (32psi front, 37psi rear), in the give-and-take of winding roads there was a certain squishy feel to the handling and too much understeer . . .

'A 2.5-litre Urraco, with its milder engine and smaller tyres, is already distinctly a "man's car" and the Silhouette is even more so. The engine is noisier and racier in character, though not crude except when it's idling or accelerating hard in the 3,000rpm range.

'Shifting the five-speed transaxle requires deliberate movements and considerable effort but is never problematic. When we got into the acceleration tests and I was trying to make the shifts as quickly as possible,

the 4-5 change became a Herculean effort that left us smiling and me rubbing my right shoulder.'

After the last Silhouette had been made, in 1978, and the last Urraco, in 1979, there was a hiatus in the manufacture of small Lamborghinis. This intermission came to an end with the 1982 revival of the Silhouette, lightly modified and carrying a new name. The car was the Jalpa, and this ultimate evolution of the Urraco was to have a six-year life ahead of it.

The first result of Giulio Alfieri's short stay with Lamborghini, the Jalpa was a response to the desperate need to introduce a car that would compete successfully with the Ferrari 328 GTS and the Porsche 911S and sell in substantial numbers.

Using a stroked 3,485cc version of the 90-degree V8, breathing through four Weber twin-choke downdraught 42DCNF carburettors, power output was 255bhp at 7,000rpm. The 267bhp

Opposite: With doors open and everything else, including the headlamps, in the raised position, the Silhouette debatably looks a bit of a mess. Rear three-quarters is the best angle at which to view the car. From here it looks neat and well-balanced; this is, after all, the view that most other motorists saw.

V8 Ferrari was heavier than the Lamborghini, the 231bhp flat-six Porsche lighter, and both proved faster than the upstart from Sant'Agata.

Compared to the Silhouette the rear decking was smoother and shapelier and the wheelarches were more substantial; the overall appearance was rather neater. Optional was a very large – and appropriately expensive – rear aerofoil. If you buy a car fitted with this, in the interests of commonsense and aesthetics it should be discarded at the earliest opportunity. The Targa top, meanwhile, remained a bit much for one person to remove and replace on

Driving the Jalpa

The Jalpa inherits the Urraco's uncanny levels of adhesion, light and precise steering and four-square roll-free tautness, but otherwise has a very different personality – thanks to that up-gunned 3.5-litre power unit.

Big-hearted and red-blooded, it has a hard-edged character – but not a roughness, mind – that reflects the greater mechanical complexity of its quad-cam configuration. Match this to the Jalpa's firmer ride on its wide low-profile rubber, and you have an altogether more aggressive package; it's just a shame the gearchange is still hardly a model of precision and that the clutch remains on the heavy side.

Lower-profile rubber gives the Jalpa a firm ride, while the bigger 3.5-litre engine dishes up a gutsy performance. (LAT)

Left: Alfieri's efforts in developing the Jalpa from the Silhouette did not extend to changing the looks, and the tacked-on front spoiler is hardly elegant. It has to be said that colour is very important, and red arguably does not suit the Jalpa as well as some other shades.

Opposite top: In contrast this Jalpa in an unusual bronze colour looks more than a little attractive.The model deserved to sell more than 179 over a ten-year period. (LAT)

Opposite below: Lamborghini worked hard at improving the Jalpa's cockpit. They failed. As one journalist commented, the instruments look as they are stuck on still in their boxes. The striped upholstery of this car looks a trifle nauseating, too. (LAT)

his or her own, and in replacing it the driver had to fiddle around aligning the rear of the roof with the locking catches before the roof could be lowered into position.

Inside, the driving position was low-slung and semi-reclined, as you would expect on a car of this type, but the leather-covered steering wheel was mounted too high – in compensation providing more legroom for taller drivers. All the same, Lamborghini should have had enough commonsense to make both seat height and the steering wheel adjustable on all models.

As with all cars of this type, visibility for the driver was not as good as it should have been. Still, at least a very real effort had been made to improve the quality of the interior finish and the leather trim of the Jalpa was executed to a very high standard – even if Lamborghini suffered its usual blind spot about the layout of instruments and switchgear. When a *Motor Sport* journalist drove one of these cars, he contrasted the high level of engineering with the poor layout of the interior:

'There is…an old saw about how deep beauty is, and under the soft alloy skin, the quality of Lamborghini

Portofino – a Lamborghini with four doors

The Jalpa provided the engine and transmission for the Portofino, a remarkable styling exercise built in 1987 and exhibited at that year's Frankfurt motor show to celebrate Chrysler's acquisition of Lamborghini.

The first four-door Lamborghini since Frua's 1978 Espada-based Faena, it had a predictably original door configuration, with no centre pillar and scissor-hinged forward and rearward opening doors. For such an arrangement to work satisfactorily, the body shell had to possess enormous strength and rigidity, and this was largely achieved by the use of specialist alloys.

The styling was the work of Chrysler's Pacifico studio, and Coggiola in Turin undertook construction; the Cd was quoted as 0.342, which is hardly a stunningly low figure. With its mid-mounted 225bhp Jalpa power unit the Portofino was claimed to have a maximum speed of 155mph; this seems rather optimistic, as a standard Jalpa was good for only about 150mph.

The Portofino was based on Jalpa mechanics and was of startling appearance, but Chrysler decided that this was a concept too far and it was abandoned not long after it had appeared at the 1987 Frankfurt show. (John Lamm)

engineering *is* beautiful. Raising the engine cover on its gas struts reveals softly shining castings enclosing the camshafts and the chains which drive them, and quadruple exhaust manifolds flowing together as smoothly as if they had been made of plasticine,' he wrote.

'It looks as if no compromises have been made, in the best tradition of Italian automotive endeavour. So it is all the more disappointing to open the long heavy door and see the ill-assorted selection of boxes in which the instruments are housed. It almost looks as if they have never been unpacked; but at least the important ones, mph and rpm, with oil pressure between them, are quite visible through the ideally sized leather wheel.

'Subsidiary gauges, three to the left and one to the right, are at times covered by a hand, but never for long, while minor functions are served by a double block of square push-buttons above the centre console. These are decorated with a selection of rather uninformative symbols, which had me peering at the block of 15(!) dim warning lights dead ahead to see whether I had switched off the fan or put on the sidelights.'

Forced to struggle against the odds, Lamborghini did its best to market both the Jalpa and the Countach in its latest form, but it was very much an uphill struggle. The Jalpa was a worthy match for both the Porsche 911 and for the Ferrari 328GTB/GTS, and on the face of matters there was not much to choose between them. The

problem was that potential purchasers were deterred by anxiety as to whether Lamborghini would be around to provide after-sale support. Both Ferrari and Porsche were so very well established in the market-place, and Lamborghini's vulnerability was, alas, common knowledge.

Of the 400 or so Jalpas built over a six-year period it is suggested that at least 50 were right-hand drive. So if rhd is a major factor in the buying process, then the Jalpa combines the attractions of a very unusual, rare Lamborghini with a good chance of obtaining one suitable for British roads. There is little doubt that a Jalpa is cheaper to maintain than a Countach and spares availability is somewhat better than with earlier cars from Sant'Agata.

Above: Head-on, the Jalpa looks formidable. A fair number of these cars were supplied with right-hand drive. (LAT)

Left: One of the obvious strong points of any Lamborghini is the engine – not just its performance but also its appearance. Mounted transversely, the V8 3.5-litre unit of the Jalpa is very neatly installed behind the cockpit. (LAT)

The LM

The LM was a Lamborghini like no other. Here is an LMA prototype, the engine by this stage having moved to the front.

The idea of a Lamborghini off-roader seems about as likely as a Lotus double-decker bus, but the massive four-wheel-drive LM (for *Lamborghini Militaria*) was indeed designed, built and sold by Lamborghini – even if precious few examples of this automotive aberration ever found a home.

To trace the development of the LM it is necessary to go back to 1977, when Lamborghini was approaching its financial nadir and was desperate for money. Negotiations had accordingly been concluded with an American company, MTI (Mobility Technology International), to develop a high-performance, all-terrain vehicle, based on a concept by N Bard Johnson of MTI. The project was intended to be a pitch for the US army's custom, at a time when the military was seeking a new super-Jeep; in the end, when the MTI-Lamborghini vehicle fell by the wayside, this emerged as the Hummer. But we're jumping ahead of ourselves, as back in 1977 MTI thought it was in with a chance, and teamed up with Lamborghini because of the Italian company's background of exceptional engineering technology.

The result was the Cheetah, a rear-engined prototype with a tubular chassis, all-round independent coil-and-wishbone suspension, and, of course, four-wheel drive. The power unit was a pushrod overhead-valve Chrysler V8 of 5,898cc developing 183bhp at 4,000rpm, coupled to a three-speed automatic transmission. The door-less body was panelled in glassfibre. After a great deal of hard work, it was exhibited at the 1977 Geneva motor show. The car was far from ready for production, and needed plentiful development.

The whole project in fact proved to be ill-conceived, beginning with its financing: as Lamborghini had no money and MTI had no substantial funds, the Italian government was persuaded to foot the bill. Then MTI found itself in the middle of a wrangle with Ford, who claimed that the Cheetah infringed the copyright of its own XR311 off-road vehicle and announced that it would be commencing legal proceedings. Neither Lamborghini nor MTI could afford to contest any such action, and the Cheetah project quietly folded, the sole prototype being written off in an accident during testing.

There had, however, been considerable interest in the vehicle, including a tentative order from the Syrian army. Accordingly during 1981 a small team of about ten worked on a development of the Cheetah in Lamborghini's prototype department. The result was a completely redesigned car. There was an all-new chassis in a mixture of square and round-section tubing, derived from

Lamborghini LM002
1986–92

ENGINE:
60-degree V12, front-mounted; light alloy construction throughout

Capacity	5167cc
Bore x stroke	85.5mm x 75mm
Valve actuation	Twin overhead camshafts per bank of cylinders, chain-driven; four valves per cylinder
Compression ratio	9.5:1
Carburettors	Six Weber twin-choke horizontal 44DCNF
Power	450bhp (SAE) at 6800rpm
Torque	340lb ft at 5200rpm

TRANSMISSION:
Four-wheel-drive; ZF five-speed gearbox with synchromesh on all forward ratios; transfer box to give alternative high and low ratios; three limited-slip differentials

SUSPENSION:
Front: Independent by wishbones, coil springs and telescopic dampers
Rear: Independent by wishbones, coil springs and telescopic dampers

STEERING:
Rack-and-pinion; power-assistance; four turns lock-to-lock

BRAKES:
Front: Girling 10-inch (255mm) ventilated disc
Rear: Girling drum
Servo-assisted, dual circuit

WHEELS/TYRES:
Steel nine-stud 17in wheels
Tyres 325-65/VR17 Pirelli Scorpion

BODYWORK:
Steel tubular cab, glassfibre panelling; four detachable doors; rear area for carrying equipment

DIMENSIONS:

Length	15ft 8.5in (4.9m)
Wheelbase	9ft 10in (3.00m)
Track, front and rear	5ft 3.5in (1.615m)
Width	6ft 8.5in (2.00m)
Height	6ft 8in (1.85m)

PERFORMANCE:
Max speed (est)   130mph
Other performance figures not available

PRICE INCLUDING TAX WHEN NEW:
Not available in the UK

NUMBER MADE:
301

NOTE: This model was also offered in the United States with a 7-litre engine, as the LM004-7000

Brief Specifications of Prototypes
LM001
1981

ENGINE:
90-degree V8 AMC cast-iron block, rear-mounted

Capacity	5898cc
Bore x stroke	101.6mm x 90.9mm
Valve actuation	Pushrod
Carburettor	Single four-barrel
Power	180bhp at 4000rpm

NOTE: this vehicle was also tested with a Lamborghini Countach 4754cc engine developing 332bhp at 6000rpm

TRANSMISSION:
Four-wheel-drive; three-speed automatic with torque converter

LMA/LM002
1982

ENGINE:
60-degree V12, front-mounted; light alloy construction throughout

Capacity	4754cc
Bore x stroke	85.5mm x 69mm
Valve actuation	Twin overhead camshafts per bank of cylinders, chain-driven
Carburettors	Six Weber horizontal twin-choke 45DCOE
Power	332bhp at 6000rpm

TRANSMISSION:
Four-wheel-drive; ZF 5-speed with synchromesh on all forward ratios; transfer box to give alternative sets of high and low ratios

Giulio Alfieri

Giulio Alfieri was born at Parma in 1924 and joined Maserati in 1953. In 1955 he became chief engineer and was responsible for the overall design of the 300S and the mighty 450S sports-racing cars, as well as later developments of the 250F Grand Prix car and the 'Bird-cage' sports-racing cars. His great years were 1956–57, when Maserati was battling to defeat Ferrari in both Formula 1 and sports-car racing and he was working with Stirling Moss (1956) and Juan Manuel Fangio (1957).

He stayed with the company throughout its difficult years from 1958 onwards, and was responsible for the design of all Maserati GT cars from the original 3500 through to the Ghibli, Indy and Khamsin and the mid-engined Bora and Merak. He was an experienced administrator and was one of the most able engineers in the Italian high-performance car industry.

Alfieri went to work as usual on the day after Alessandro de Tomaso took control of Maserati on 8 August 1975, only to find that he had been dismissed and his personal effects were stacked up in the car park. De Tomaso felt obliged to shed the company's most experienced and able member of staff, simply because he was the one man qualified to challenge the Argentinian's authoritarian rule.

After Lamborghini was placed in receivership, the receiver Alessandro Artese obtained the consent of the court to bring in Alfieri to run the company. He managed to keep production going steadily, albeit at a

Giulio Alfieri, one of the most able and experienced Italian automobile engineers, seen at Sant'Agata during his years with Lamborghini under Mimram ownership. (Author's Collection)

lower than economic level; when there was no cash for wages, he would fund these from his own pocket. When the Mimrams took over Lamborghini, Alfieri stayed with the company as chief engineer.

British magazine *Car* interviewed Alfieri shortly after it had been announced that the Mimrams had bought the factory. Alfieri told the journalists that a car design was like a painting: the best men had their own techniques and should not be influenced in any but the most general way by their peers.

'Technically speaking,' he said, 'I have never seen a Miura. I had not

seen a Countach until I came here to Lamborghini. If you ask me about the layout of the current Ferraris, I cannot tell you.

'When Dallara designed the Miura with its transverse 12-cylinder engine, he brought great merit on himself – Lamborghini had shown great responsibility in building it. I had done a transverse 12-cylinder car at Maserati in 1961, using the 1.5-litre Formula 1 engine, but as an answer to the Miura I still thought the Ghibli [a front-engined V8 of 4,719cc/4,930cc] was right. Perhaps it was an older solution, but for the time I thought that it was good enough and I still don't believe I was wrong. We built 1,000 Indys [the four-seater sister car to the Ghibli] alone.'

At Lamborghini, Alfieri was responsible for the Silhouette, the 5-litre production versions of the Countach, and the LMA and LM002 all-terrain cars. It has been said that Alfieri's preoccupation with the LM002 was his downfall. Certainly, it did not prove the great success that Alfieri and the Mimrams believed it would be. After the Chrysler takeover, Alfieri took early retirement at the age of 64 and received a fairly generous pension.

It is most likely that Chrysler believed that younger men of broader outlook should run Lamborghini and that his retirement did not represent any substantial adverse criticism of his work at Sant'Agata. Giulio Alfieri died on 19 March 2002 at the age of 78, one of the most highly respected men in the Italian motor industry.

existing drawings, and suspension front and rear was now by torsion bars, working in conjunction with enormous tubular dampers and 16in wheels. Two engines were tried: the 4.75-litre Countach V12, developing about 300bhp, and a 5.9-litre AMC V8, still rear-mounted and mated to a three-speed Chrysler automatic

gearbox and a transfer case for the permanent four-wheel drive. Lamborghini proposed to fit the most sophisticated radio equipment and, as the car was intended mainly for sale in the Middle East, it was to have the most powerful possible air-conditioning. There was a very large nose skid-plate and an electric winch

at the rear, and it was intended that the body would have two, four or no doors, according to the user's requirements. Despite an estimated weight of about two tons, it was calculated that the new LM001 would have a maximum speed of 120mph.

By 1982 the prototype had been completely redesigned and was now

Left: In 1977 Lamborghini exhibited the rear-engined Cheetah all-terrain vehicle at the Geneva show. As seen here, it was in doorless form and had a very utilitarian interior. The project was abandoned, only to come to life again. (LAT)

Below: The front-engined LMA fully equipped for desert use, with a roll-back cover on the seating area and a jerrycan at the rear.

Genesis – a Lamborghini MPV!

If the LM seems alien to Lamborghini's traditions, a further stretching of marque values – even if only in theory – was the Genesis show-car of 1988. Dreamt-up by Bertone and displayed at the 1988 Turin show, the Genesis was nothing less than a Lamborghini-based MPV. With a mid-mounted Countach V12 and a gullwing front canopy incorporating the windscreen, this bizarre creation had sliding rear doors and an unusual horizontal split to the side glazing. The stylists responsible were Marc Deschamps for the exterior and Eugenio Pagliano for the interior.

The Genesis has an essentially clean profile, dominated by the unusual glasshouse treatment with its sweeping horizontal dividing spar. Below left: The entire front opens up gullwing-fashion around a central hinge-point. The rear doors slide open and shut. Below right: The interior features three rows of seats, despite the mid-engine configuration. (Bertone)

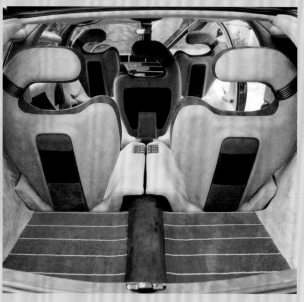

Lashings of leather and wood characterise the LM cabin, which is dominated by the huge girth of the central tunnel. (LAT)

known as the LMA – for A*nteriore* or 'front' – and subsequently as the LM002. The most significant difference was that this latest version had the engine, now the 4.75-litre Countach V12, mounted at the front: this made the handling safer and increased load capacity at the rear. The four-wheel drive was now selectable, and the transmission was by a ZF five-speed manual gearbox, with the transfer box offering high and low ratios, to give a range of ten gears; limited-slip differentials were standard on both front and rear axles. The front hubs free-wheeled until locked manually for off-road use.

There were three very substantial roll-bars within the cabin area, but despite this it was said that the maximum carrying capacity was 11 people. The body remained in glassfibre, with detachable doors, and the overall impact was of a very big, bulky vehicle, with generally square lines. Maximum speed was quoted as 120mph, as before, and the LM002 could ascend a gradient as steep as 1-in-1.2 – or so it was claimed. Among the proposed list of optional extras was a machine-gun mount…

There is no doubt that the Mimrams

and Giulio Alfieri had great confidence in the LM002 and saw it as a substantial source of income. Sales manager Ubaldo Sgarzi reckoned that a production line turned over to the model would enable Lamborghini to build 90 cars a month. This was a delusion: throughout development the Mimrams and their staff consistently over-estimated the likely demand for such a vehicle. In any case, the LM002 was not yet ready for production and delays were to diminish the sales prospects further.

Eventually, the definitive LM002 entered production in 1986 and was built in small numbers until as late as 1991. Most of the problems had been ironed out and the only real differences between this and its prototype predecessor was the use of drum rear brakes and – for most cars – the fitment of a 5,167cc version of the Lamborghini V12 engine; the model was also available with a 7.3-litre unit developing 420bhp at 4,500rpm and evolved from a powerboat engine. In this form the car was known as the LM004-7000. With such propulsion it is hardly surprising that the fuel tank had a massive 62-gallon capacity…

Such was Lamborghini's confidence

in the LM002 that they contracted with Spanish coachbuilder Irizar to supply the chassis and body in unpainted form and agreed to take delivery of 500 units. By the time that Chrysler took control of Lamborghini, it was obvious that this vastly exceeded Lamborghini's needs and the contract was negotiated down to 300 body/chassis units, which equated approximately to the total number of vehicles built.

Lamborghini sold the LM002s to two distinct markets, these being Middle East armed forces and a small number of private owners – presumably those who appreciated having what was, in the memorable words of Brock Yates of *Car and Driver*, 'the closest thing to a street-legal Tiger tank'. For private use the standard configuration was four seats (more like armchairs, and covered in soft leather) and two more side-facing dickey-seats on the poop deck with its guardrail, behind the cabin. These 'civilian' cars also had a thick-rimmed Nardi steering wheel and bits of wood were glued on in appropriate places to give an impression of quality.

There were certain aspects of design that Lamborghini rarely got right, and

Opposite above: The eventual production version, the LM002, was introduced in 1986 and was built in small numbers until 1992. The engine is now mounted at the front, there are wheels of a different style and the appearance is even more rugged. Opposite below: Powering the LM002 is the Countach QV engine developing 450bhp; transmission is by a five-speed gearbox connected to a two-speed transfer box giving ten forward gears.

fully down to standard were the poor driver's visibility (in the case of the LM002 thanks to the enormous bulge over the Weber carburettors inhibiting the view) and the casual scattering of instruments and switchgear.

The clutch was incredibly heavy and had to be fully depressed to achieve a clean gearchange, while the change itself was also on the heavy side. This made the LM002 an extremely tiring car to drive. Lamborghini claimed a maximum speed of 125mph and acceleration from 0–60mph in 8.5 seconds, but as far as I am aware no journal has fully tested an LM002 and produced a set of figures under proper conditions. The factory figures, including single-figure fuel consumption, seem about right, all the same.

The LM002 is in any case a totally unsuitable vehicle to drive on the road. It is a car for deserts, mountain ranges and tundra. Equally, its use for military purposes was thwarted by its complexity and the inherent unsuitability of a quad-cam engine for cross-country work.

Consequently many military vehicles were soon unloaded onto wealthy private owners, some of who used them for hunting in the desert. But if the LM002 holds little appeal to the ordinary lover of classic cars, it would however seem an eminently suitable vehicle for a maharajah's tiger-hunting. With rifles and searchlights mounted on the roof, and servants ensconced on the poop deck, it would have proved much more practical than the Rolls-Royces traditionally used for this purpose. Sadly, there are now very few maharajahs and very few tigers left.

The LM002 cabin gives seating for six and another two passengers can be carried in the rear on side-facing dickey-seats.

The Diablo

The Diablo in its final 6.0SE form. Note the restyled front with exposed rather than pop-up headlamps. (LAT)

The Diablo appeared 17 years after the first production Countach and was to prove even more successful. Diablo, Spanish for devil, is supposed to have been the name of one of Spain's most famous fighting bulls. Whether that is true or not, I do not know, but there has always been a lot of 'bull' about Lamborghini names.

The Diablo was the first completely new car designed by chief engineer Luigi Marmaroli to go into production at Lamborghini. Marmaroli had joined Lamborghini from the unsuccessful Alfa Romeo Formula 1 team in January 1985. He came to Sant'Agata with a specific brief: to develop a new car that was coded the P132. Initially he worked on the Countach 'Anniversary' and then turned his attention to what was to become the Diablo. The company approached a number of outside designers and the proposals

Diablo and Diablo VT
1990–98

ENGINE:
60-degree V12, mid-mounted longitudinally; all-alloy construction

Capacity	5729cc
Bore x stroke	87mm x 80mm
Valve actuation	Twin overhead camshafts per bank of cylinders; four valves per cylinder
Compression ratio	10:1
Fuel system	Weber-Marelli electronic port fuel injection
Power	492bhp (SAE) at 7000rpm
Torque	428lb ft at 5200rpm

TRANSMISSION:
Rear-wheel drive; five-speed Lamborghini gearbox with synchromesh on all ratios; optional VT four-wheel drive, with up to 25 per cent of power transmitted to front wheels Final drive 2.41:1; transfer ratio 1.59:1; effective final drive ratio 3.83:1

SUSPENSION:
Front: Coil springs and double wishbones, spring/damper units; anti-roll bar
Rear: Coil springs and double wishbones, twin spring/damper units each side; anti-roll bar

STEERING:
Rack-and-pinion; no power assistance until 1992; 3.2 turns lock-to-lock

BRAKES:
Front: 13in (330mm) ventilated discs with Brembo aluminium-alloy callipers
Rear: 11.2in (285mm) ventilated discs with Brembo aluminium-alloy callipers
Servo-assisted, dual circuit

WHEELS/TYRES:
Cast alloy five-stud 17in wheels; 8.5in rims at front, and 13in at rear
Tyres 245/40ZR-17 front and 335/35ZR-17 rear, Pirelli P Zero

BODYWORK:
Two-door coupé (roadster available from 1995) with steel tubular frame; aluminium-alloy and carbonfibre/glassfibre composite panels

DIMENSIONS:

Length	14ft 8.6in (4.46m)
Wheelbase	8ft 3.3in (2.65m)
Track, front	5ft 0.6in (1.54m)
Track, rear	5ft 4.5in (1.64m)
Width	6ft 8.3in (2.04m)
Height	3ft 7.5in (1.10m)

WEIGHT (KERB):
32.4cwt (1,646kg)

PERFORMANCE:
(Source: *Road & Track*)

Max speed	202mph (estimated)
0–60mph	4.5sec
0–100mph	10.8sec
30–50mph in top	5.5sec
50–70mph in top	5.7sec

(Last two figures from *Autocar* test of GT model, 1999)

PRICE INCLUDING TAX WHEN NEW:
£160,000 (Diablo VT, 1994), rear wing £2,300 extra
£195, 461 (GT, 1999)

NUMBER MADE:
There is no precise figure because of the destruction of records during Indonesian ownership of the company. The figures below are not necessarily precisely accurate. Some sources claim that total production amounted to about 3,300 cars including the 6-litre version.

Diablo and Diablo VT	2,097
Diablo SE	150
Diablo Roadster	85
Diablo SV	184
Diablo SVR	50
Diablo SV Roadster	34
Diablo GT	80
Diablo GTR	30
Total	2,655

Diablo 6.0-litre
2000–01

As 5.7-litre Diablo except:
ENGINE:

Capacity	5992cc
Bore x stroke	87mm x 84mm
Compression ratio	10.7:1
Power	550bhp at 7100rpm
Torque	457lb ft at 5500rpm

TRANSMISSION:
VT four-wheel-drive as standard

WHEELS/TYRES:
Alloy 18in wheels, front and rear

DIMENSIONS:

Length	14ft 8in (4.47m)
Track, front	5ft 3.4in (1.61m)
Track, rear	5ft 5.7in (1.67m)
Width	7ft 2.7in (2.20m)

WEIGHT (KERB):
32.0cwt (1,624kg)

PERFORMANCE:
(Source: *Motor Trend*)

Max speed	205mph (estimated)
0–60mph	3.4sec
0–100mph	8.4sec
30–50mph in top	Not available
50–70mph in top	Not available

PRICE INCLUDING TAX WHEN NEW:
£155,000 (2000)

NUMBER MADE:
383 (including 45 SE versions)

---

of Marcello Gandini, now running his own design office, were accepted. As early as June 1988 Gandini had produced a full-scale styling exercise.

The first prototype was tested at Nardo in the spring of 1989, with a much-developed 5.2-litre version of the Countach engine. After these tests Lamborghini concluded that the new car lacked sufficient top speed, despite the fact that it was more powerful and more aerodynamic than the Countach. It was therefore decided that the Lamborghini V12, still basically the same Bizzarrini design of 1963, should be redeveloped. Chrysler, who had taken control of Lamborghini in April 1987, also requested substantial changes to the body shape, in particular to the rear panels round the air intakes. These modifications were carried out in Chrysler's Detroit studios under the direction of Tom Gale, vice-president for design. The Diablo re-emerged later in 1989 in 5,729cc form and with substantially modified styling. Chrysler now approved the mechanical side of the design, but requested further changes to the bumpers and engine cover. Despite the difficulty in satisfying the bosses in Detroit, Gandini was content after all this for his signature to appear in facsimile on the car's flanks.

As before, the V12 was installed

This cutaway of the Diablo in VT four-wheel-drive form was published in 1990, although this version was not available until 1992. The Diablo is a very complicated design, but it was conceived and executed with considerable thought. (LAT)

longitudinally, with its nose to the rear of the car. In its original 5.7-litre form, the Diablo's engine, with redesigned and stiffer castings, and with the camshafts now driven by a single-row chain with automatic tensioner, developed a mighty 492bhp at 7,000rpm – almost 40bhp more than the Countach unit. The fuel system integrated the electronic ignition with a sequential multi-point electronic Weber-Marelli port injection system (known as LIE). Lamborghini built only one version of the engine, with a full three-way catalytic converter and Lambda sensor, to suit all markets.

Linked to this impressive power unit was a redesigned five-speed gearbox, projecting well into the cabin of the car and with a short remote linkage to put the gearlever in the most convenient position. The output shaft of the gearbox stepped the power to the right side of the car and rearwards through a short driveshaft running alongside the engine sump – as oppposed to on the Countach, where this shaft ran through the sump. The differential housing was integral with the sump housing.

Although a natural progression from that of the Countach, the chassis

incorporated significant changes. As previously, it was a welded space-frame, but now it was of square and rectangular-section tube throughout, and designed to spread the loadings throughout the structure. The type of tubing used also made the attachment of components much simpler.

The Diablo was also designed from day one to be built in four-wheel-drive form and this added both weight and bulk. Steel of very high strength was used to construct the cockpit and at front and rear the steel of the spaceframe was designed to absorb engine stresses.

The coil-spring independent suspension used welded tubular-steel double wishbones and was derived from that of the Countach, but now incorporated anti-dive and anti-squat geometry and an additional transverse link at the rear. Another change was that rubber bushes were used at the pick-up points to reduce road noise and harshness, whereas the Countach had its suspension mounted rigidly on the body. Originally power-assisted steering was not offered, but it was standard from 1992. An omission was ABS brakes: apparently the reason was that Lamborghini could not

Opposite top: To celebrate the 30th anniversary of the company, Lamborghini introduced the very limited-production, very special Jota version of the Diablo in 1994. It is a superb-looking car in its metallic mauve finish. Lamborghini claimed a maximum speed of up to 205mph and 0-60mph in four seconds.

Bottom: With the Diablo the interior presentation of Lamborghinis took a major leap forward. (LAT)

persuade manufacturers to supply these for such a low-volume car.

Over the years the shape of the Countach, originally regarded as somewhat bizarre, had become accepted, even if few would class it as beautiful. For the new model Gandini took his original design parameters, moved them on 20 years, and produced an aerodynamic shape of grace and beauty, with smooth-flowing lines, no exaggerated aerodynamic devices and far neater detailing than on its predecessors. The door glasses were now one-piece and fully opening, with quarter-windows behind.

The shape of the body flowed through high wings to a neat vertical tail. Between the rear wings there was

Driving the Diablo

On the road the Diablo is easier to drive than a Countach, but it can still be very hard work. It is not a nimble car, and lighter and more lithe machinery can run rings round it on twisting and mountainous roads. Although easier to drive, it is also still not a car that is happy around town or in heavy traffic.

With greater torque than almost any other car of its time, the engine is more flexible than that of the Countach and the power delivery is consistent throughout the engine speed-range without any flat-spots.

When driven spiritedly, some ride and roadholding shortcomings do become apparent. In particular over bumps and badly-surfaced roads in and around town the suspension thumps excessively, while at speed over the crests of slopes and hills the front of the Diablo can suddenly feel disconcertingly light.

The Diablo's natural environment, though, is the open road, where it retains fantastic grip through corners and the massive brakes, despite the

absence of ABS, are superlative under all conditions. The acceleration is of course phenomenal and the car thrives on semi-racing starts: set the car at a steady 4,000rpm (the engine note changing from a grumbling rumble on tickover to a frantic roar), drop the clutch, and the enormous rear tyres grip and you're away.

There are still two Lamborghini faults. One is exceptionally heavy steering at speeds below 60mph. This is not an issue, of course, on cars with power steering, although some might feel the powered set-up lacks the feel present on other very high-performance cars with power steering.

The other area where the Diablo falls short is the gearchange, which seems unduly heavy. It should also be said that by the time that the car was on the market many rivals including Porsche were offering close-ratio six-speed gearboxes, and some might feel short-changed by this omission on the Diablo.

As has become traditional with Lamborghini, the gearlever of the Diablo works in an open gate; many commentators still thought that the gearchange was too heavy. The general quality of fittings is higher on the Diablo than on earlier cars from Sant'Agata. (LAT)

a heavily-louvred engine cover, but it was low enough to allow reasonable rear vision. The aerodynamic spoilers front and rear blended neatly into the bodywork and although the nose seemed a little on the high side, the company pointed out that this was necessary to comply with United States regulations that the bumper be a minimum of 20 inches above the ground. A rear wing was optional and in the UK cost an extra £2,300.

The Diablo was a bigger car than the Countach, with a 6in (150mm) longer wheelbase and it was both a little wider and longer overall. Weight rose by about 350 pounds (159kg), because of the need to incorporate electric windows, air-conditioning and a high-quality sound system that could be heard above the mechanical and exhaust noise of the V12 engine. An undertray helped to reduce

aerodynamic lift at high speeds.

For the body Lamborghini used light alloy for the doors and quarter panels, but the engine cover, bonnet and bumpers were constructed in carbonfibre/glassfibre composite, as was the central tunnel over the gearbox, which – as on the Countach – projected well forward into the cockpit. The interior was vastly improved, with beautifully finished high-quality leather upholstery, the gearchange working in a Ferrari-style open gate, and the steering wheel adjustable for height and reach. The layout of the instruments was much better, in a neat cowled panel, with larger speedometer on the left, tachometer on the right and the minor instruments between them.

As usual there was a central panel for switchgear, but the layout was clear and intelligently laid out. There

was no longer space for luggage behind the engine, as this area was occupied by the exhaust system and catalytic converter. Instead, Lamborghini made provision for a small quantity of luggage at the front of the car and an optional extra was a set of fitted luggage that filled this 5cu ft space – roughly the size of an original Mini's boot, but only this generous because the spare wheel had been discarded.

To put it very simply, in its final form the Diablo was a very satisfactory motor car; it was satisfactory to both Lamborghini and Chrysler and to the buying public, even though it never sold in the numbers anticipated.

Soon the regular Diablo was joined by a 4wd version called the VT (for 'Viscous Transmission'), and announced at the 1992 Geneva show. The basic transmission layout

Above: Powerhouse! The 5,992cc engine in the very last Diablo produced. A massive 590bhp at 6,800rpm is quoted by Lamborghini. (LAT)

Left: The channelled rear deck is striking – just don't expect good visibility. (LAT)

Below: Later Diablos lost their concealed headlamps. (LAT)

Above: The view of a Diablo that you're most likely to see. Dramatic and sculptural, it is far cleaner in its lines than the last of the Countaches. (LAT)

Right: In comparison with the 'biscuit-tin' scoops of the Countach, the air intakes on the Diablo are beautifully shaped – or is this a case of 'organic' versus 'techno'? (LAT)

remained unchanged, but a propshaft incorporating a viscous coupling ran forward to a differential unit at the front, set up so that the front wheels were driven only when the rear wheels started to spin. Both front and rear differentials were of the limited-slip type; at the rear there was a 45 per cent locking factor and at the front one of 25 per cent.

Lamborghini selected the front and rear axle ratios so that the front and rear driveshafts ran at the same speed, thereby avoiding slip in the viscous coupling when the car was driven in a straight line at a steady speed. Power-assisted, speed-sensitive steering was standard on the VT and at the same time was incorporated on the regular Diablo.

So far as the vexed question of maximum speed is concerned, Lamborghini claimed 202mph for both 2wd and 4wd versions, but no magazine had the opportunity of confirming this and they all thus relied on estimates. All that can be said is – and it means very little – is that if the Diablo were allowed to reach its peak

Diablo SVR: for Gentlemen Racers . . .

In 1996–97 Lamborghini sponsored the Lamborghini Class Challenge, with professional and amateur categories. All competing cars were the SVR model developed for racing, on much the same lines as the VTR cars sold in Japan; 'SV' stood for *Sport Veloce*. Power output was 540bhp at 7,100rpm and in racing trim the cars weighed 27.6cwt (1,400kg); maximum speed was said to be 186mph. Lamborghini sold 50 of these cars over two years, which represented a major boost in production.

LeasePlan France sponsored the series of races and provided a two-year lease facility, including all running expenses and accident damage. The cost was £175,000, about £125,000 being for the car, and the leasing arrangement entailed an up-front payment of £13,500 and then £5,000 per month over two seasons. At the end of this period the driver/hirer kept the car. All the races were in Europe and the series started in 1996 with a supporting race at Le

Mans, followed by events at circuits such as Nürburgring, Anderstorp, Brands Hatch, Spa-Francorchamps and Nogaro. In one-hour races the 'gentleman' driver was allowed to share his car with a professional. The series ultimately continued until 1998. While it helped Lamborghini and gave the marque good publicity, the races were of no real significance. One of these cars in full 'warpaint' is in the Lamborghini museum.

Above: The SVR competition version of the Diablo. Note the outline of the bull painted on the nose and side. Lamborghini built 50 of these cars to compete in a series of races held in 1996-97 and the French LeasePlan company offered a special deferred payment system for would-be racers. Below: Two SVRs in action. By modern competition-car standards the cars were cheap to buy, and a special deal covered race preparation and accident-damage repair. But what could you do with the car after the series, apart from put it into a museum?

of 7,400rpm in top gear, this would equate to 216mph.

Lamborghini's claimed top speed was higher than that of 194mph billed by Ferrari for its Tipo 512 Testa Rossa. If Italian manufacturers considered they could claim that they built the world's fastest car on the basis of unproven figures, they were disabused when a Jaguar XJ220, a very *limited* production car, achieved a genuine 213mph at the Nardo test track in Italy. Lamborgini's response was the SE Jota (see below).

In normal driving conditions, there was very little difference between an ordinary Diablo and the VT version, but at higher speeds the VT was inherently the safer and easier car to drive, as when traction was lost at the rear, up to 25 per cent of the power was transferred to driving the front wheels. An additional and important feature of the VT was electronically-staged damping. The softest setting firmed up at about 80mph, became firmer still at about 120mph and assumed its hardest setting at 155mph. These settings could also be selected manually, should one so wish.

Above: A cockpit view of the Diablo GT. Although beautifully laid-out and finished to very high standards, the aubergine colour of the trim does rather scream at the yellow exterior. Racing-style seats are fitted to this model. (LAT)

Right: Another feature of the GT is 18in forged alloy wheels finished in black. (LAT)

Opposite: The 6-litre Diablo GT, another limited-production model, was introduced in 1999. There was a choice of gearing, and the rear wing was an optional extra. In its ultimate form Lamborghini claimed a maximum speed of 210mph. The company has an unfortunate tendency to paint press and demonstration cars yellow, which arguably does not show them off at their best. (LAT)

During the long production life of the Diablo, there were many variations and short-run models to boost sales. The first of these was the Diablo SE introduced in 1993 to celebrate the 30th anniversary of the marque. This special-equipment version had air-conditioning as standard and an engine developing 520bhp at 7,100rpm. To avoid type approval

Opposite: The Diablo roadster was a bold initiative. This view shows the sophisticated aerodynamics of the Diablo tail and emphasises the very forward seating position of these cars. Above: Lamborghini's transformation of the Diablo from coupé to roadster is neat. One of the big problems in building very high-performance open cars is avoiding cockpit turbulence at high speed.

tests, the extra equipment was offered in the form of 'optional extras'. Claimed maximum speed for the Diablo SE was 205mph.

Derived from the SE was the SE Jota, which had power boosted to a claimed 600bhp at 7,300rpm. To tame this, traction control and adjustable anti-roll bars were fitted. Above all, weight was reduced as much as possible, measures taken including deletion of the air-conditioning, electric windows and even the cigarette lighter and ashtray. Other changes included panels, dashboard

and seats in ultra-light carbonfibre.

Additionally there were 18in cast magnesium-alloy wheels and other changes were louvred rear slats as on the Countach and an adjustable rear wing. The car was said to weigh 28.6cwt (1450kg). Lamborghini claimed a top speed of 207mph but muddied the waters when factory technicians openly talked of having achieved 220mph. The precise number built is not known, but there were very few, as the Jota was never intended as a serious production car. Gérard Larrousse built up a Lamborghini based on the Jota for racing in Japan. It had a specially commissioned chassis, although it retained the general outline of a Diablo.

Supplementing the closed Diablos was the roadster that first appeared in prototype form at the 1992 Geneva show, complete with a cut-down windscreen and no provision for a hood. The production car of 1995

onwards had a detachable Targa top that could be stored neatly on top of the engine cover. This top consisted of two carbonfibre sheets filled with insulation and weighed only a few pounds. Mechanically, the Roadster was the same as the standard Diablo. Because of the destruction of Lamborghini's records, the total production is not known for certain, but is believed to be over 100. Claimed maximum speed was 201mph.

The Diablo SV, meanwhile, was introduced for 1996, and had a power output of 500bhp at 7,000rpm. As the result of suspension development, it handled much better than earlier cars. Production included two cars delivered to Japan modified for GT racing. In this form power output was 540bhp at 7,100rpm and the cars were designated the VTR; they achieved some success in Japanese racing. There was also a limited run of

Because of aerodynamic necessities, the tail of the Diablo VT Roadster has a rather cluttered appearance. This sequence shows how the car's look changes dependent on whether the roof is in place . . . stowed on the rear deck . . . or removed altogether.

Right: Pretty in pink? The two-tone interior of this Roadster is certainly . . . striking.

roadsters to SV specification, with very low lines thanks to a cut-down windscreen which meant that the car could only be used in open form.

Two late-life variants were the Diablo GT and its competition derivative the GTR. The former was introduced at the Frankfurt motor show in 1999 following the acquisition of the company by Audi. Engine capacity was increased to 5,992cc and power output was 575bhp at 7,300rpm. The car was offered with a choice of gearing and wing configuration, and quoted maximum speed thus varied between 200mph and 210mph. It should be noted that from 1999 onwards all Diablos had fixed headlamps of Nissan origin…

The Diablo GTR competition model also introduced in 1999 featured a modified 5.9-litre engine developing 590bhp at 7,300rpm. Weight was reduced by about 1.8cwt (90kg) and Lamborghini claimed a maximum speed of 210mph. Private teams raced these cars in Europe, the United States and also in Australia, and once again there was a special series for these cars; they also competed in Endurance Championship racing, including appearances in the Nürburgring and Spa 24 Hours races.

The Raptor: Diablo in a Zagato suit

It's tempting to think that Zagato's Diablo-based 1996 Raptor was just another extreme showcar. True, it was extreme. True, it was a one-show wonder, being exhibited at the 1996 Geneva *salon* and then largely disappearing from view. But the Raptor was in fact intended to be a limited-production catalogued model.

The idea was that of Swiss Lamborghini and Zagato enthusiast Alain Wicki, who acted as middleman in a project to bring the two firms together for the first time since the 3500GTZ. Prompted by then Lamborghini president Mike Kimberley's interest in creating some special-edition models, the idea was to offer a modular body that could have add-on elements to transform it for road or track use as appropriate – hence the one-piece hinge-up cockpit section.

The basis was a strengthened Diablo VT four-wheel-drive chassis, with its accompanying mechanicals, and the skimpy body enabled dry weight to be slashed to 26.6cwt. The car was a fully-engineered runner, and whatever one might think of its looks, it was a tempting enough prospect to prompt 550 expressions of interest from would-be customers.

But then the Raptor became caught up in the last days of the Indonesian regime at Lamborghini, while Zagato suddenly seemed to lose interest. When Audi took over it was hoped the new team at Sant'Agata might take up the project, but nothing came of this. Eventually a disillusioned Wicki sold the car at auction.

The aggressive front end of the Raptor features a gaping air intake. Below: The rear treatment evokes the classic 'double-bubble' Zagato roofline, while the engine-cover slats pay homage to the Miura. Bottom: The sides and canopy lift as one – shades of Bertone's Giugiaro-styled 1963 Testudo, amongst others. (LAT)

So devilish that you'd want to sell your soul? An evocative night shot of a Diablo SV by top photographer Tony Baker, of Classic & Sports Car magazine. (LAT)

In Australia, Paul Stokkel drove a GTR with considerable success in the GTP Nations Cup series.

Mention should be made of another racing Diablo. This was built in the UK by the AIM team and had a specially-commissioned chassis and re-arranged mechanicals so that the gearbox was at the extreme rear, in the manner of most mid-engined competition cars. The works ostensibly gave permission for the construction of this car and it was to have had factory-developed engines. It ran at the Le Mans test day in 1995 and looked promising, but then a wrangle broke out between the sponsors and Lamborghini. It appears that permission had not come from the top and Lamborghini's Indonesian owners succeeded in having the project stopped.

Buying Hints

1. Early Diablos in particular are noted for their clutch problems. The clutch isn't man enough for the job, and a life of 15,000 miles is about average – especially if the car has been driven irresponsibly or the clutch has been ridden. Worse, clutch replacement is not always carried out properly, especially when it comes to the correct adjustment at the slave cylinder.

2. Don't be surprised – or worried – if a Diablo has had a replacement crownwheel-and-pinion set. Early cars suffered from failure of the pinion spline, so it's good to know this problem has been tackled. Check, though, that the work has been carried out by a reputable specialist.

3. On early Diablos the hydraulic timing-chain tensioner was prone to failure. Remember to listen for a noisy chain at tickover, disappearing as the engine is revved. Most cars will have been given a mechanical tensioner.

4. As with the Countach, the Rose joints of the anti-roll bar tend to rattle when worn, and the clamp brackets can develop play.

The Murciélago

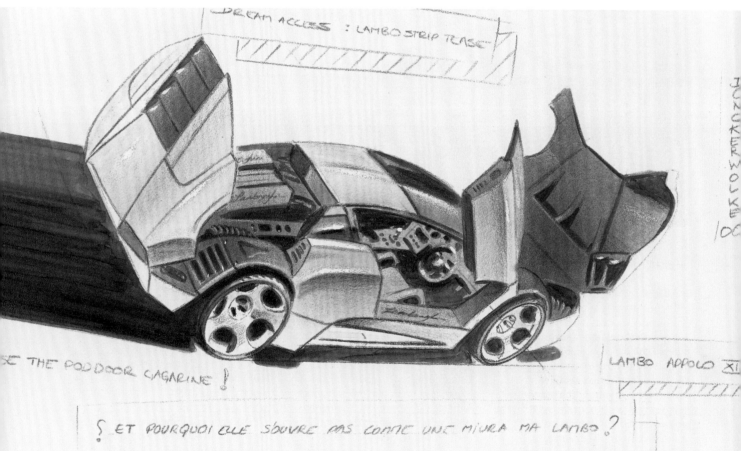

This wonderful Donckerwolke sketch plays with the idea of one-piece Miura-like front and rear panels. Jokingly captioned 'Lambo Appolo [sic] XIII', the drawing asks the question – in French – 'Why shouldn't my Lambo open up like a Miura?'. The writing to the left reads 'Close the pod door Gagarine' – a reference to Soviet astronaut Yuri Gagarin (or Gagarine in French).

Italian inspiration, German execution: in some ways the Murciélago is the dream supercar, refining the Countach theme without losing the soul of the dramatic original. Scissor-doored, tubular-framed and V12-powered, its DNA is not in doubt, but there's a new polish to design and presentation – without this getting in the way of the usual searing performance.

When Audi completed the acquisition of Lamborghini, the reactions of management and employees was very mixed. Under Indonesian control, the company had developed and put into production the Diablo, but finance had been lacking

Murciélago
2001 to date

ENGINE:
60-degree V12, mid-mounted longitudinally; aluminium-alloy construction throughout

Capacity	6192cc
Bore x stroke	87mm x 86.8mm
Valve actuation	Twin overhead camshafts per bank of cylinders; four valves per cylinder
Compression ratio	10.7:1
Engine management	Lamborghini LIE management unit and electronic multi-point sequential port fuel injection; drive-by-wire throttle
Power	580bhp (SAE) at 7500rpm
Torque	479lb ft at 5400rpm

TRANSMISSION:
Four-wheel drive; Lamborghini six-speed gearbox with synchromesh on all ratios; viscous coupling limited-slip differentials front and rear, with front allowing 25 per cent slip between each wheel and the rear allowing 45 per cent slip between each wheel; traction control

SUSPENSION:
Front: double wishbones, coil springs, electronically-controlled dampers; anti-roll bar
Rear: double wishbones, twin coil springs and electronically-controlled dampers; anti-roll bar

STEERING:
Rack-and-pinion; power assistance; 3.5 turns lock-to-lock

BRAKES:
Front: 13.2in (355mm) ventilated disc
Rear: 13.2in (355mm) ventilated disc
ABS anti-lock software

WHEELS/TYRES:
Aluminium-alloy five-stud 18in wheels; 8.5in front rims and 13in rear rims
Tyres 245/35 ZR18 front and 335/30 ZR rear, Pirelli P Zero Rosso

BODYWORK:
Two-door two-seater coupé, steel tubular frame with steel roof and carbonfibre panels
Two-seater roadster available from late 2004

DIMENSIONS:

Length	15ft 0.3in (4.58m)
Wheelbase	8ft 8.9in (2.665m)
Track, front	5ft 4.4in (1.635m)
Track, rear	5ft 6.7in (1.695m)
Width	6ft 8.5in (2.045m)
Height	3ft 8.7in (1.135m)

WEIGHT (KERB):
35.9cwt (1,823kg)

PERFORMANCE:
(Source: *Road & Track*)

Max speed	205mph (estimated)
0-60mph	3.6sec
0-100mph	8.7sec
30-50mph in top	Not available
50-70mph in top	Not available

PRICE INCLUDING TAX WHEN NEW:

Coupé	£170,000 (2004)
Roadster	£190,000 plus extras

NUMBER MADE:
Not available, as current production model, but see Chapter 14 for information as to production levels. It is known that 1247 had been built as at the end of 2004, plus 65 Roadsters.

Murciélago Roadster
2004 to date

As coupé except:

BRAKES:
Front: 15in (380mm) ventilated discs with eight pistons
Rear: 13in (355mm) ventilated discs with four larger pistons

DIMENSIONS:

Height	3ft 6in (1.065m)

WEIGHT (DRY):
32.8cwt (1665kg)

The frontal aspect of the Murciélago is clean and aerodynamically efficient.

to press ahead with production of the Bravo and financial investment was erratic. There was no cohesive plan for the future direction of the company. It had been yet another disquieting period in the company's history.

There was no doubt that Audi would give the company financial stability and an assured future, but there were apprehensions that German control would impose on the workforce a regimen that would prove unacceptable to the less self-disciplined Italian mindset and that the cars would become too Audi-influenced and lose their traditional Italian bravura and character. To date those fears have proved totally groundless.

Although it was necessary for the Diablo to remain in production until 2001, Audi's prime concern was to develop and put into production its successor as speedily as possible. The design of the new car, to be known as the Murciélago, had been settled by early 2000 and thereafter Lamborghini concentrated on construction of the first prototypes and development testing. In all there were eight pre-production prototypes and they were tested extensively as well as being used for crash-testing and type approval in the USA, the EU,

Canto: False start on replacing the Diablo

Believed to have been an early prototype for the successor to the Diablo, the Canto, code-numbered L147, was seen only in spy shots taken during testing on the high-speed banked Nardo testing circuit in 1998. The Canto retained the 6-litre version of the Lamborghini V12 engine (with modifications) and had a completely new body of startling lines, with the rear wings sweeping upwards to form small tail fins. Zagato was responsible for the body, which was largely built of carbonfibre composites.

Changes to the engine were reported as including variable valve timing, a variable-length induction system and a drive-by-wire throttle – all of which features were to appear on the Murciélago. Transmission was said to be by a new six-speed gearbox – again, this was adopted on the Murciélago – and with close ratios it was reckoned that the Canto would top 200mph. There was talk of the Canto appearing at the 1999 Geneva show, but this did not happen: the car was being developed during the time that Audi was negotiating for the acquisition of Lamborghini, and the German firm had other ideas for the future of the marque.

Right: The Murciélago 6.2-litre V12 engine has mighty power and torque curves. Below right: The engine bay is very neat and is well shrouded.

Switzerland and Japan.

Construction of the body of the first prototype was sub-contracted to two comparatively small engineering firms in Turin. Following delivery of the chassis and bodyshell to Sant'Agata in June 2000, the company was able to submit the prototype for approval at Audi's technical centre at Neustadt in early July. Approval of the design was forthcoming and after this full development testing started. Without Audi resources, it would have been impossible to achieve production status by October 2001 and it is also remarkable that a car developed so quickly has proved such an excellent all-round package.

The Murciélago was named after a bull that fought so valiantly in 1879 that its life was spared and it retired to Don Miura's estancia where it fathered a long line of fighting animals. Murciélago is also Spanish for a bat.

Just as the Diablo followed the basic layout of the Countach, so the Murciélago – and it now seems appropriate, for a current model, to use the present tense – has followed the layout of the Diablo, but again with significant changes. The engine remains the basic Bizzarrini design of 1963, but capacity has been increased to 6,192cc, and power output is a

Above: At the rear a good external appearance has been achieved without detriment to aerodynamic stability.

Right: Seeking influences from the past, this artwork features two startling Gandini concept cars for Bertone, the Alfa Carabo of 1968 (centre) and the Lancia Stratos of 1970 (bottom).

Record-breaking at Nardo

In February 2002 Lamborghini went record-breaking with a Murciélago to the Italian Nardo test track, with a view to establishing that it was the world's fastest production car then available by taking the FIA-sanctioned overall world hour record for production cars. The attempt was held in gusty conditions and at the wheel was test driver Giorgio Sanna. One of the problems facing the team was the fact that the Murciélago could not run for a full hour with the standard fuel tank at full throttle. The rules did not permit the fitting of a larger tank.

The left front tyre chunking off bits of tread also plagued the attempt, something not experienced during the many tests conducted at the circuit. Sanna completed 13 laps of the 7.83-mile track before stopping – this despite the tyre problem. After a refuelling stop and a tyre change, Sanna completed the hour, but, of course, the tyre change had caused delays that reduced the speed. The Murciélago achieved the following

from a standing start:

One hour:	189.548mph
100 kilometres:	198.859mph
100 miles:	199.002mph
Fastest lap:	202.552mph

One might say that this means very little because the previous one-hour record stood to a turbocharged 2-litre Saab at about 140mph, but the exercise does have its interesting aspects. Since the appearance of the Countach more than 20 years ago, journals have rarely been able to measure the maximum speed of a 'big' Lamborghini, quite simply because of the lack of suitable facilities. The record-breaking car was in totally standard form and it was running on a banked circuit (and thus a higher speed could have been obtained if a long enough straight had been available). We now know that a standard Murciélago is good for over 202mph and that the claimed maximum speed of 205mph is almost certainly no exaggeration.

stupendous 580bhp at 7,500rpm, while dry-sump lubrication has permitted its installation 2in (50mm) lower in the chassis. Each of the four camshafts has an actuator that varies valve timing so as to provide improved throttle response and also reduce exhaust emissions. Electronic sequential port fuel injection is retained, and there is a drive-by-wire electronic throttle. Another important change is the introduction of a Variable Airflow Cooling system. The two large radiators are positioned at the rear of the engine compartment and are fed through channels by flaps. These air intakes pivot upwards 20 degrees to draw in more air; they can be moved by pressing a button, but also move automatically according to the needs of engine cooling. With the flaps open, the drag coefficient is increased from 0.33 to 0.36. The point has been made that with these flaps open the car does look rather like a bat – and, as mentioned above, that is the strict meaning of the model's name.

There is of course power assistance for the steering and the massive brakes have a computerised ABS anti-lock system. This system is of the so-called DRP (Dynamic Rear Proportioning) type that ensures

Left: The interior of the Murciélago is stylish and of the highest quality without being fussy. The instruments are laid out in a single cluster. The gearchange operates in an open gate – unless you specify the e-Gear paddle shift.

Below: In a medium-blue metallic the Murciélago looks very different.

Opposite: The lines of the Murciélago are well balanced, uncluttered and unmistakably those of a Lamborghini.

optimum distribution of braking forces between front and rear wheels. The specification of the engine reflects the latest technology, but the result is a car that is easier and more responsive to drive and much of a driver's anxiety about *how* he is driving the car is removed. In addition, because of the engine changes, the V12 idles much more smoothly.

A major change is a new six-speed gearbox; the gearchange still operates in an open gate, but with the important difference that there is a straight change from first to second gear, with reverse tucked away up at the top left of the gate. The new gearbox has the primary and secondary layshafts running on three bearings. This ensures steady, rigid operation of both the gearlever and the internals of the gearbox. Because of double and triple-cone synchronisers, the gearchange is more precise and considerably lighter than on previous Lamborghinis. Under previous ownerships, there had been constant complaints about the heaviness of the change, but nothing was ever done.

The Murciélago has permanent four-wheel drive as standard, using the same central viscous coupling. Again there are limited-slip differentials front and rear, with the front differential allowing 25 per cent slip between each wheel and that at the rear 45 per cent. According to the situation, between 28 per cent and 80 per cent of the torque can be delivered to the front. The Lamborghini LIE electronic management system provides traction control by limiting the amount of torque available and also modulates the drive-by-wire throttle and the fuel injection/ignition. The driver is able to turn off the traction control, if he wishes.

Driving the Murciélago

The first thing to strike one with the Murciélago is how in Audi ownership Lamborghini has made vast strides in the quality of interior trim and in the logic of the layout of instruments and switchgear. The beautifully-stitched Italian leather (cut from skins in the factory) exudes quality and luxury, as well as smelling great. This material covers almost the whole of the cockpit. All the instruments are set within a large binnacle behind the steering wheel and all are clearly visible, while there is no longer a bewildering array of switches and the controls for the radio and the air-conditioning are now within close reach. By moving the front suspension mounting points forward a little, too, footwell space has been slightly increased.

It has to be remembered that the Murciélago is a big, heavy car. The Diablo was bigger than the Countach, but the latest model is four inches longer than its immediate predecessor and because of all the additional equipment is around 3.6cwt (181kg) heavier. It is very much

a *grande routière* in the traditional sense of being a very high-performance touring car with a truly outstanding performance on well-surfaced not too winding roads and being immensely comfortable for two people – but not nimble or at its best on difficult terrain.

Certainly the straight-line performance is unmatched: not even the Ferrari 575 Maranello is as fast, although in mitigation it is somewhat cheaper. And what more can you want than a car that will achieve 62mph in first gear, 89mph in second, 121mph in third, 157mph in fourth, and 181mph in fifth – with a further 20mph still to come in top? Apart from the straight-line performance, the Murciélago has truly exceptional brakes, largely neutral handling with a slight tendency to understeer, brilliantly responsive steering and, at long last, a first-class gearchange.

At one time the weight distribution of 42:58 front-to-rear would have been a recipe for a disastrously oversteering tail-happy monster, but so much has changed through

Driving the Murciélago is an intoxicating experience.

modern suspension technology and the Murciélago handles with the docility of a poodle and the response of a well-trained border collie. The acceleration is truly explosive, as those enormous Pirelli tyres bite into the tarmac, and is accompanied by the rumbustious roar of the engine, but even that is somewhat modulated compared with Lamborghini engine sounds of yesteryear.

Inevitably, fuel consumption is enough to frighten the ordinary driver. The Murciélago averages about 12mpg and with a 22-gallon tank the safe touring range is about 250 miles – not enough for such a fast car. In realistic terms the big Lamborghini is not a car for everyday use, and every Murciélago owner needs another more practical car. It is a brilliant car to drive within the limitations already mentioned, but, of course, at a very heavy price. That price many will consider well worth paying . . .

Top: A characteristic feature of recent and current Lamborghinis has been the large forward-hinged doors. On the Murciélago they do not cut deeply into the roof, so in wet weather the interior is kept as dry as possible when the doors are opened. Compared to those of the Diablo, they rise by a further five degrees. Above left: The very neat front lights and the beautifully cast alloy wheels of the Murciélago. Above right: Although the side intakes drawing cooling air to the brakes and engine are rather prominent, they blend in well with the overall styling and break up what would otherwise be a somewhat featureless profile.

Luc Donckerwolke

Born in Lima, Peru, on 19 June 1965, Belgian Luc Donckerwolke worked for Peugeot before joining Audi as a stylist in 1992. Between 1994 and 1996 he worked for the VAG-owned Skoda company before returning to Ingolstadt. He became styling co-ordinator at Lamborghini in September 1998, and worked on the styling of the Murciélago and Gallardo, for which cars he won the 2003 Red Dot Award.

He is now in charge of Centro Stile Lamborghini, the company's recently opened design studio, and at the time of writing had just designed the roadster version of the Gallardo, scheduled for release in 2005. He is also working on a possible third model for the Lamborghini range, the introduction of which is firmly linked to the rising sale of existing models and the input of further substantial finance from Audi.

'It was like a dream and I didn't know when I would wake up,' said Donckerwolke of his move from Skoda to Lamborghini, speaking in an interview with *Classic & Sports Car* magazine.

Luc Donckerwolke, head of styling at Lamborghini.

'I decided to enjoy every minute. I was conscious that there was no excuse for failing to fire emotions for the fanatics. It was a point of no return.

'At the launch of the Murciélago, I seriously considered stopping being a designer and training for another career – I was sure that I would never be involved with such an intense and fantastic project again. Then they asked me to take responsibility for the future of Lamborghini design…

'I want to eliminate ornamentation and vulgarity and concentrate on more serious, formal treatments – the orchestration of curves like the hips and *taille* [waist] from a feminine body…

'The golden rule (when designing a Lamborghini) is to identify the DNA in order to extrapolate the future. I tried on the Diablo 6.0 and GT to introduce some of the changes coming with the Murciélago. The hard task is to produce, in three dimensions, the emotions of the seven deadly sins [pride, wrath, envy, lust, gluttony, avarice and sloth], playing with the forbidden to create objects that let you forget about rationality.

'I don't want to restrict myself to formal design language. It's important that you can recognise a Lamborghini from any other car from 150 metres away. Every model should cultivate the extreme in its segment.'

Above: The intake flaps adjust automatically in response to cooling needs – with manual override possible.

Opposite: Although the Murciélago roadster is a very beautiful motor car for the exceptionally wealthy, it is not entirely practical. Recommended maximum speed with the hood in place is a relatively modest 100mph.

As with past Lamborghinis, the chassis is a tubular steel structure, but the floor is fabricated from carbonfibre and the rest of the structure incorporates carbonfibre and honeycomb attached by rivets and adhesive. The roof and body panels are steel. Front and rear the suspension is independent by double wishbones, with coil springs, together with an anti-roll bar, and incorporates anti-dive at the front and anti-squat at the rear. The dampers are Koni FSD ('frequency selecting dampers'), which are not electronic but are self-adjusting depending on the frequency of movement. There are four settings and they can be adjusted manually, but the automatic system is so good that there is little point. According to Lamborghini technical director Massimo Ceccarini these dampers

help lift the ride/handling of the Murciélago – and of the Gallardo – to 'a new level.'

Since its launch various Murciélago derivatives have been announced. The first was the R-GT unveiled at the 2003 Frankfurt motor show. A new competition model developed jointly by Audi and Reiter Engineering, it was intended for sale to private owners to race, primarily in the GT category. The most important technical change was a reversion to rear-wheel drive only. Weight was slashed to about 21.7cwt (1,100kg) and a large rear wing dominated the R-GT's appearance. The prices of competition cars have always been deliberately vague, but Lamborghini talked of a price of 'under 500,000 euros', which is roughly equivalent to £350,000.

Early in the 2004 season Reiter

Engineering fielded one of these cars in the Valencia GT race. It should have won, but finished third because of a mishap at the start. The R-GT failed to fire up, either because a fuse had fallen out (the official story) or because the rather bulky driver had knocked off the master switch. After a delayed start the Lamborghini went superbly well.

Although it appears that collectors bought other examples, six cars were sold for racing. The Krohn-Barber team in the United States bought two, but quickly withdrew from racing; the British DAMS team, which had been at the forefront of Formula 3000 in the late 1980s, raced two that were owned by collectors; and in Japan the Japanese Lamborghini Owners Club raced two cars in partnership with Amprex.

The next variant to appear was the Murciélago Roadster announced at the Geneva show in 2004 and entering production in the summer of that year. There are substantial differences between it and the coupé. Styling chief Luc Donckerwolke substantially restyled the new car and evidently part of the aim was to make the Roadster look as aggressive as possible. Features include streamlined headrests incorporating 'mobile' air vents, a reshaped tail with the engine cover hinged at its trailing edge to improve accessibility, and an electronically controlled roll-over bar that operates automatically, emerging from its housing behind the seats 'in only a few milliseconds during a roll-over emergency', according to Lamborghini. The height is lower

and a soft top can be fitted. Lamborghini intends the Roadster as a fair-weather car and with the top in place the maximum recommended speed is 100mph.

There have been structural changes to the chassis and to increase rigidity there is a lattice brace in the engine compartment, in steel as standard but available at extra cost in a visible carbonfibre version. Further aiding stiffness, the construction of the cockpit glazing has been designed to integrate with the structure of the vehicle.

The Roadster has its own style of aluminium-alloy wheel, pierced at the base of each spoke, and larger brakes are fitted. An automatic system enables the front axle to be raised by 1.8in (45mm) at low speeds, which may give some comfort on very bumpy

Opposite and above: The Murciélago R-GT is a lightweight racing version announced in 2003; drive is to the rear wheels only, and there are extensive aerodynamic addenda.

surfaces, but it does seem unlikely all the same that one could drive a Roadster without grounding it from time to time. The standard gearbox is the six-speed manual, but the six-speed 'e-Gear' automatic gearbox with paddle shift is optional – as it has been on the regular Murciélago since 2003.

Lamborghini built only 65 of these cars in 2004, mainly for the United States market, but the aim is that production should rise so that half of all Murciélagos built are Roadsters. This in itself is a very strong hint that the buyer of a Murciélago is not purchasing serious everyday transport.

The Gallardo

Overall the Gallardo's styling is rather neater than that of the Murciélago; although a much smaller car, it is clearly a member of the same family.

Opposite: The Gallardo with doors, boot and bonnet open makes an aesthetically pleasing sight, but one does hope that not many buyers will choose this particularly violent shade of yellow.

At last! After many years of hesitations and upsets, Lamborghini now has a spiritual successor to the Urraco – a more compact and at least modestly more affordable alternative to the Murciélago.

The company's plans to introduce a new, smaller-capacity car had survived several changes of management and it was a policy that Audi wanted to pursue. Various styling exercises had been carried out and the intention had been to use engineer Luigi Marmaroli's proposed 72-degree V10 engine. The reality, though, was that Audi had inherited a project without a policy. Fortunately, however, Lamborghini's new owners were certainly not lacking in management skills, so the situation was salvageable, and the Audi-led team's aim was to challenge and beat the technical performance of the main competition, the ageing Ferrari 360 Modena and the Porsche 911 Turbo.

Massimo Ceccarini, who had been with Lamborghini since the days of the Mimrams and was Marmaroli's deputy, had become chief engineer following the departure of Marmaroli during the

Lamborghini Gallardo
2003 to date

ENGINE:
90-degree V10, mid-mounted longitudinally; aluminium-alloy construction throughout

Capacity	4961cc
Bore x stroke	82.5mm x 92.8mm
Valve actuation	Twin overhead camshafts, chain-driven; four valves per cylinder
Compression ratio	11:1
Engine management	Lamborghini LIE management system and electronic multi-point sequential fuel injection
Power	492bhp (SAE) at 7800rpm
Torque	376lb ft at 4500rpm

TRANSMISSION:
Four-wheel drive; six-speed Graziano gearbox with synchromesh on all forward ratios; automatic e-gear paddle-shift transmission optional. VT 4wd features 45 per cent limited-slip at rear; at front, slip limitation is by ABD function. Final drive 3.077:1

SUSPENSION:
Front: Coil springs and double wishbones, combined spring/damper units; anti-roll bar
Rear: Coil springs and double wishbones, combined spring/damper units; anti-roll bar

STEERING:
Rack-and-pinion; power assistance; 3.1 turns lock-to-lock

BRAKES:
Front: 14.37in (365mm) ventilated discs with eight-piston callipers
Rear: 13.2in (335mm) ventilated discs with four-piston callipers
ABS anti-locking software, with ESP full stability-control system

WHEELS/TYRES:
Alloy five-stud, 19in wheels; 8.5in front rims and 11in rear rims
Tyres 235/35 ZR19 front and 295/30 ZR 19 rear, Pirelli P Zero Rosso

BODYWORK:
Two-door coupé; alminium-alloy monocoque, aluminium-alloy panels

DIMENSIONS:

Length	14ft 1.3in (4.30m)
Wheelbase	8ft 4.8in (2,56m)
Track, front	5ft 3.9in (1.622m)
Track, rear	5ft 2.7in (1.592m)
Width	6ft 2.8in (1.90m)
Height	3ft 9.9in (1.165m)

WEIGHT (KERB):
29.9cwt (1,520kg)

PERFORMANCE:
(Source: *Autocar*)

Max speed	192mph
0-60mph	4.1sec
0-100mph	9.0sec
30-50mph in top	9.4sec
50-70mph in top	8.1sec

PRICE INCLUDING TAX WHEN NEW:
£117,000; paddle-operated e-gear transmission £7,600 extra

NUMBER MADE:
2148 to the end of 2004

Top left: The front lights are set in narrow vertical units, giving the Gallardo a very different look from the Murciélago. Top right: Whereas the Murciélago has a twin exhaust system, with the pipes emerging together, on the Gallardo a single exhaust exits on each side of the car. Above: The sculpted rear features L-section lamps that integrate beautifully with the vent above and the grille below.

period of Indonesian ownership. He retained this role following the acquisition of Lamborghini by Audi. His brief was to work closely with the Audi technical centre in developing the new smaller car – to be called the Gallardo, after one of the five original breeds of Spanish fighting bull.

An early key decision was that the engine would remain a V10, universal in Formula 1, and adopted for production by Dodge for the Viper and later by Porsche for its Carrera supercar and BMW for its M5. It would not, however, be Marmaroli's V10, but a new engine with the cylinders at an angle of 90 degrees. The 72-degree layout was abandoned because the centre of gravity would have been higher and, in Ceccarini's words, 'the package would have been compromised.' Apart from any other factor, rear vision would have been inhibited.

What has emerged is a dry-sump

5-litre V10 engine derived from Audi's V8, using the same basic block design, with the same bore centres and the same chain-drive for the four overhead camshafts. The design has however been extensively redeveloped, changes including new variable-geometry induction, variable intake and exhaust valve timing, redesigned pistons, and a new exhaust manifold. Throttle control is 'drive-by-wire', with two electronic throttle bodies, and the Gallardo has its own engine management system, developed in-house.

There is also a new 18-degree crankshaft to ensure even firing. In simple terms, V8s and V12s are easy to balance and there are few problems in achieving smooth running, but with V6s and V10s it is much more difficult. As on the Murciélago and its predecessors the engine is mounted longitudinally, back to front, in the chassis.

For the Gallardo, the design team commissioned Graziano to develop and build a new six-speed gearbox specifically for this model and this is mounted behind the engine. The Graziano company, one of the new breed of specialist transmission builders, also supplies gearboxes to Ferrari, Maserati and Aston Martin. There is the choice of a conventional manual gearbox or Lamborghini's own version of the paddle-operated Magnetti Marelli electronic gearbox – Lamborghini reckons that its form of electronic gearbox is smoother than the rival from Maranello because of the superior software and ECU developed at Sant'Agata.

At the time of the Gallardo's 2003 introduction, incidentally, there was comment about the failure of the new Lamborghini to use the VAG Group's dual-clutch transmission, as fitted to Golf-based models such as the Audi TT. The answer was that at the time this system was suitable only for cars with transversely-mounted engines and no version for cars with longitudinally-mounted engines had yet been developed.

As on the Murciélago, the Gallardo has four-wheel drive using the VT

The V10 engine is derived from an Audi unit. Power is 492bhp, with a hefty 376lb ft of torque at 4,500rpm.

Driving the Gallardo

Murciélago performance in a smaller package, with a chassis that offers both security and comfort, the whole built to German standards: that's the Gallardo in a nutshell.

The V10 might have a slightly odd beat, relative to Lamborghini's V12, but it shares the 12-cylinder car's strong low-down torque, effortless revability and annihilating performance – along with its own very distinctive soundtrack. This seductive

engine is mated to a chassis that is sportingly firm – low-profile rubber aiding this – yet blessed with sufficient wheel travel to keep the Gallardo firmly planted to the tarmac even when road surfaces are at their worst. With four-wheel drive, adhesion is never an issue, and for any normal mortal the car simply stays stuck to its line.

The six-speed manual gearbox is slick, but marred slightly by a high

take-up point for the clutch, and the brakes are as meaty as you have a right to expect. With power steering now an inevitable standard fitting, there is less feel at the helm than there could be, however: old hands might lament the loss of the raw communication offered by – say –- a Miura's elemental unassisted rack. But times move on, and by any standards the Gallardo is a profoundly impressive achievement.

Above: The rear of the Gallardo is nicely unfussy.

Right: The interior of the Gallardo is finished to a high standard but is very basic, with a minimum of instrumentation. Note the flattened base to the dished steering wheel. This is a car with the e-Gear electronic change, operated by paddles either side of the steering wheel.

system, with limited-slip differentials front and rear. One of the problems in using the VT system is the added weight, this being some 220 pounds (100kg). It is the prime reason why there has been so much effort to make other aspects of the Gallardo as light as possible.

Thus aluminium-alloy is used for the spaceframe chassis, which is derived from the original Lamborghini design but is of more advanced conception and has exceptionally high torsional stiffness. A German company, Krupp-Drauz, a regular supplier of components to Audi, builds these chassis and delivers them complete with aluminium-alloy body panels, in white primer, to the Neckarsulm plant of Audi. Here they are painted and then delivered by lorry to Sant'Agata.

The wishbone suspension is also constructed from aluminium-alloy. As on the Murciélago, the shock absorbers are the Koni FSD type. Power-assisted rack-and-pinion steering is standard. As always on recent Lamborghinis the ventilated disc brakes are immensely powerful and the latest and most sophisticated anti-lock system is fitted. There are twin water radiators at the front and an oil cooler at the side.

One of the most satisfactory features of the Gallardo is the styling of the body. Lamborghini had sought design proposals from Audi itself, Bertone, Giugiaro's Italdesign and IDEA. Zagato, who had made such a hash of the Raptor body, was not invited to submit proposals. Ultimately the only one that appealed was Giugario's design, although in Donckerwolke's hands it was substantially altered. In particular, 'wrapover' rear lamps replaced the round ones of the original design and Donckerwolke added a discreet but highly effective rear spoiler and altered the shape of the air intakes. Ceccarini estimates that only 30–40 per cent of the final design is attributable to Giugiaro. Although there is a very clear, indisputable family relationship between the bodies of the Gallardo and the Murciélago, the V10 is much smaller (the engine, in particular, is a very snug fit), it has rather squarer lines, and it has conventional doors.

Partially because of these doors, coupled with a sensible interior layout, the Gallardo is an immensely pleasurable car to drive. Although the sills are still wide, the driver can easily and comfortably slide across the seat into a driving position that is adjustable electrically, as is the steering column. The driving position is well to the front of the car, but even tall drivers are now accommodated in real comfort – on a rather thinly padded seat that gives better support than its appearance would suggest. The clutch action is a little awkward, but the gearchange is fine, as is the power steering, although the latter lacks feedback.

The instruments are again in a cowl behind the nicely dished steering wheel, all are clearly visible, and the Audi-sourced switchgear is well positioned in the central console and clearly marked. This is a car in which the driver rapidly feels completely at home. As the figures indicate, the performance is superb, and so is the roadholding, with a slight bias towards understeer. Adhesion is remarkable and the ride is firm, but very comfortable.

Turning to practicalities, a criticism is the lack of luggage space, with there being just room for a few items behind the seats and a small soft bag in the nose. Lamborghini intends the Gallardo to be a car suitable for everyday use, but omissions of this kind mar its usability.

At a 2005 price of £117,000 the Gallardo is considerably dearer than its closest rivals, the Ferrari 360 Modena (£103,275) and the Porsche 911 Turbo S (£99,300). There is little doubt that Lamborghini wanted to price the car well clear of its rivals to make a point about its quality. However, although there is a three-year unlimited mileage guarantee, the likely high cost of repairing these cars does give cause for alarm: when a Lamborghini service centre advertises an 'introductory offer' of a Gallardo clutch replacement for £3,000, then one does worry about the cost of supplying and fitting other replacement parts, the likely life of a Gallardo clutch (after all, the model has only been on the market two years), and the stupidity of manufacturers in making their cars so difficult to work on. If that is less than the standard price, it amounts to a deterrent to purchasing one of these otherwise excellent cars.

The Gallardo at speed – a very fine fast touring car with impeccable manners and handling.

The Lamborghini
factory
& museum

Following the takeover of Lamborghini, Audi carried out substantial work to extend and modernise the factory inside and out.

Audi's acquisition of Lamborghini was accompanied by a detailed assessment of future needs. Rodolfo Rocchio became chairman, but Vittorio di Capua remained chief executive and likewise Massimo Ceccarini remained head of engineering. It is undoubtedly the case that Ceccarini has far less scope for exercising discretion than he did under the Indonesian management. That said, while Audi keeps very tight control on expenditure, it does have the resources and the willingness to direct them towards new projects and developments. In 1999 di Capua retired and was succeeded by Giuseppe Greco as managing director and deputy chairman. Greco has vast motor industry experience and spent not far short of 40 years with Fiat Auto.

Although it was built 40 years ago, the Lamborghini factory is still surrounded by green fields and Audi was able to acquire additional land. It

The term 'hand-built' means very little in modern production terms, but the Murciélago has components (especially the trim) made by craftsmen, and craftsmen assemble it.

has completely rebuilt the frontage of the factory to provide a showroom, a museum and administrative offices. In modern, heavily-glazed style, the appearance has been transformed from the original and typically 1960s brick building with its small windows.

Additional building has taken place in the factory area, but much of this remains as it was in Ferruccio Lamborghini's day. There are two production lines, one for the Murciélago and one for the Gallardo.

All car factories these days are in effect assembly plants, but far more craftsmanship goes into the Murciélago than into even the most expensive of its rivals. While all the manufacture of major components is sub-contracted to companies in Italy, craftsmen (and women) operate at workstations positioned along the production line – for example the ladies cutting and preparing the leather trim from the skins, sitting at their sewing machines.

Production of the Gallardo is much more mechanised and as has been mentioned the painted body/chassis units are received directly from Germany. The mechanisation permits a greater weekly production and is the main reason for the lower price of the Gallardo. Lamborghini currently has the capacity to build ten Murciélagos a week and 25 Gallardos, but it is clear that the large assembly area is under-utilised, as it has been throughout Lamborghini history.

Lamborghini in Formula 1

Although Chrysler never intended to run its own works team in Formula 1, they did hope to be able to supply engines to constructors who would prove competitive and – just as importantly – would be able to pay for them. At Sant'Agata there were considerable doubts about the viability of this project and other aspects of Chrysler's plans, but Detroit was adamant.

Lamborghini Engineering SpA was set up, but quite who set it up is somewhat debatable. What seems to have happened is that this new company was established before Mauro Forghieri joined the team, with Emile Novaro as President. When Forghieri joined Lamborghini Engineering, he became *de facto* managing director and then put in place the organisation. Although Forghieri is a brilliant engineer, he is not an engine specialist, but more of an engineering and racing director. He persuaded two colleagues from Ferrari to join him.

Forghieri ran the engineering company from Modena and all casting and machining, together with assembly work, was contracted out, mainly to companies in Modena. It seems that Chrysler did not want the Formula 1 project conducted in-house, although the reasons for this decision are unclear – unless it was considered that it would prove a distraction to those working on the production cars.

By the end of 1988 the Formula 1 engine was ready for testing on the dynamometer. It was an 80-degree V12 of 3,493cc (85mm x 51.3mm), tagged Tipo 3512. At this time Formula 1 was for cars powered by 3,500cc unsupercharged engines. By 1989 Lamborghini claimed that it was developing in excess of 600bhp at 13,000rpm, and it seems that the maximum power achieved was around 650bhp. All the same, more development work would have been needed to make the Lamborghini

engine competitive with the Honda units used by McLaren and the Renaults of the Williams team.

As negotiations with both McLaren and Williams foundered, only smaller teams, limited on funding and running less than top-line chassis, used the Lamborghini engine – and the sort of money they could afford failed to justify continuing intensive development. In fact, these teams sometimes had difficulty in meeting their bills for the overhaul of engines between races.

Gérard Larrousse's team was the first to use these engines in 1989–90, but for 1991 it lost its sponsorship and could no longer afford the Lamborghini V12. By 1992 Larrousse had become Venturi, sponsored by the French car company of that name, and again used the ever-improving Lamborghini engines. Success was limited to sixth place by Bertrand Gachot at Monaco, although Ukyo Katayama ran as high as fifth in Canada before retiring because of engine failure.

Among the users in 1990 was Lotus, who installed the V12 in its 102 chassis (during 1989 the Lotus 101 had used

Belgian driver Eric van de Poele in his Lamborghini 291, during qualifying for the 1991 Spanish Grand Prix at Barcelona. Neither he nor team-mate Nicola Larini managed a place on the starting grid. (LAT)

the Judd V8 engine that was lighter, but less powerful). By this time Lotus had lost its competitive edge, despite sponsorship from Camel, and drivers Derek Warwick and Martin Donnelly had mediocre seasons. The best performances were Warwick's sixth place in Canada and fifth in Hungary. A new consortium took over Team Lotus for 1991, but the budget was even tighter and the team staggered through the year using Judd engines.

Another user of Lamborghini engines was the French Ligier team, which had acquired its engines from Larrousse when his team ran into financial difficulties. Ligier had enjoyed some great moments during its history, but 1991 was not one of them, despite sponsorship from France's government-owned Gitanes cigarette company. The Ligier JS35s, and the 35Bs introduced during the year, were simply not fast enough. Ligier succeeded in obtaining more substantial sponsorship for 1992 and switched to the latest state-of-the-art Renault V10 engines.

There was an interesting project to run cars with both engine and chassis built by Lamborghini. The project originated as the GLAS, sponsored by a Mexican industrialist, and Lamborghini was gulled into a deal whereby Chrysler underwrote the budget (said to be $25 million) until the Mexican's funds were in place. By the time the cars were ready at the start of the 1991 season, the Mexican had disappeared and GLAS foundered.

Carlo Patrucco, head of the Italian Fini food and hotel group, together with business colleagues and associates, stepped in and agreed to back the project, which now ran as Team Modena Lamborghini. Sadly, these cars, known as the Lamborghini Tipo 291 and driven by Nicola Larini and Eric van de Poele, were off the pace all season, and the team was wound up at the end of the year. Minardi was another team short of money that ran Lamborghini

engines in 1992–93 and the best performance was a sixth place by Christian Fittipaldi in the 1992 Japanese Grand Prix.

Another Lamborghini project with the 3.5-litre V12 engine in 1990 was a car developed for endurance racing by the works and British concessionaire Portman Garages. Spice Engineering built what was said to have been a compact, light and potentially highly competitive chassis at their Silverstone base. The project foundered when Spice Engineering went into receivership before the car could be raced.

After what was little more than a series of disasters, Mauro Forghieri left the company and when Mike Kimberley joined as president, shortly after the sale by Chrysler, Lamborghini Engineering was put into liquidation.

The Lamborghini V12 racing engine installed in the Lotus 102 chassis. Despite strong efforts by the company, no competitive team ever used the Lamborghini Formula 1 engine. (LAT)

After Werner Miscke became the new chairman of Lamborghini in 2003, he spoke guardedly to the motoring press of future plans for Lamborghini. 'We have to build up the business,' he said. 'Maybe in seven to ten years we can be selling 3,000 cars a year. We need to sustain volumes and that means derivatives. We need open versions as well as coupés. We have to discuss a third model, and a decision will be made later this year.'

Already the Murciélago Roadster is in full production, the Gallardo roadster should appear in 2005, and the competition version of the Murciélago has already appeared and raced with success – with the competition version of the Gallardo about to be launched. As for the new third model to appear under Lamborghini ownership, little is known. It does seem that the Murciélago and the Gallardo are a little too closely positioned in the market, so there is a possibility that Lamborghini will introduce a 3-litre car, perhaps rather expensive for its engine size, but built in larger numbers than either of the two current models.

Apart from Werner Mischke, the other members of the board of Automobili Lamborghini Holding SpA are Dr Martin Winterkorn, chairman of Audi and president of Lamborghini; Salvatore Cieri, chief executive officer; Massimo Ceccarani, director of research and development; and Klaus-Peter Körner, production director.

In June 2004 Lamborghini published some interesting statistics about the company. While Audi owns 100 per cent of the shares of Lamborghini, the Sant'Agata company has three subsidiaries: Automobili Lamborghini SpA (the car manufacturing company), Motori Marini Lamborghini SpA (the company that manufactures marine engines), and Lamborghini Artimarca SpA (the licensing and merchandising company). The total number of employees is 714, and the factory site occupies 100,000 square metres of which 28,900 square metres is covered by buildings.

Mauro Forghieri on the Lamborghini F1 engine

Mauro Forghieri was technical director for Ferrari from 1962 onwards and was responsible for the design and development of Formula 1, sports prototype and competition sports cars through to 1984; he left Ferrari in 1986.

Initially I was contacted by Emile Novaro, who was president of Lamborghini, and Danielle Audetto, who had joined the company as director of public relations and sports activities. As a result of this I met Lee Iaccoca, president of Chrysler at the 1987 Geneva motor show (*a month before the Chrysler takeover of Lamborghini was completed*).

Iaccoca proposed that I should join Lamborghini to design a Formula 1 engine/gearbox unit that would be competitive against such teams as Ferrari and McLaren. There was never any intention for Chrysler to run its own works team. I came to an agreement with Iaccoca and I formed Lamborghini Engineering, based in Modena and completely independent,

Mauro Forghieri photographed in his Ferrari days, in the pits in 1984.

although financially supported by Lamborghini and Chrysler.

I believe that my V12 design had considerable potential, but the problem was that only uncompetitive

teams ever raced it. Among its advantages were comparatively low costs and simplicity, but in some ways it was innovative, for example in using ceramics for ducting. We supplied an engine for test purposes to McLaren and Ayrton Senna's comments were very favourable, but McLaren decided to use another engine. We had discussions with Frank Williams of Williams, but these negotiations came to nothing because of Chrysler's financial difficulties.

Ultimately, the only teams to race the engine were Larrousse-Lola, Lotus, Team Modena and, later, Minardi. The finances were run on the basis that they made payment per engine supplied and also paid for engineering support. We had a number of other projects under way, including an electric van built from composite materials. These projects ended because of Chrysler's financial problems and I left Lamborghini in 1993.

According to the current owners, production over the last few years has been as follows:

Year	Production
1996	211
1997	209
1998	213
1999	265
2000	296
2001	297
2002	424
2003	1,305
2004	1,592

This clearly shows the vast difference in output following the introduction of the Gallardo. Turnover in the same period has been:

Year	Turnover
1996	34 million Euros
1997	38.2 million Euros
1998	37.7 million Euros
1999	47.2 million Euros
2000	60.7 million Euros
2001	64.6 million Euros
2002	93 million Euros
2003	200 million Euros
2004	243 million Euros

The main markets for Lamborghini cars are:

United States	35 per cent
Germany	20 per cent
UK	12 per cent
Japan	10 per cent
Switzerland	10 per cent
Italy	5 per cent

In the supercar class there is now a battle for decisive superiority between the two major marques, Ferrari working under the inspiration of Luca di Montezemola, who transformed Maranello's Formula 1 team in the 1970s, and Lamborghini, guided and controlled by Audi. If there is to be – in the long term – only one winner, my feeling is that Lamborghini will come out of the present wrangle as supreme, with

Ferrari relegated to number two in the supercar stakes.

It is an interesting fact that many of the world's biggest manufacturers have absorbed some of the greatest top-drawer motoring names. BMW owns Rolls-Royce, Fiat owns Ferrari (and, less importantly, Maserati) and Ford owns Aston Martin; VAG, meanwhile, seems to be split, in historical terms, between two empires, equivalent to the Roman Empire of the West and the East, with Volkswagen controlling Bentley and the revived Bugatti, and Audi overseeing Lamborghini.

The Japanese do not seem interested in this sort of prestige-gathering exercise, while General Motors . . . well, it owns Daewoo. Further takeovers seem unlikely, as there is precious little left to take over among independent, prestigious manufacturers.

The Museum

To enjoy the Lamborghini museum, you do really have to be a complete obsessive for the make. It is a fairly recent addition, attached to the right of the main building, and is on two very airy, spacious floors, with a good selection of past models and room for many more in the future, complemented by a display of engines, photographs and models. It might be said that Lamborghini lacks sufficient history to fill a museum, but even so there are surprises and the museum certainly broadens the visitor's knowledge of Lamborghini in both Formula 1 and powerboat racing.

There are 40 or so exhibits that change from time to time. Without doubt the star of the display is the original Scaglione-styled 350GTV, which has been beautifully restored. Other exhibits include a superb Miura, the first and last examples of the Countach, and a range of Diablos that traces the evolution of the model; these include the 1992 prototype roadster, and examples of both the SVR competition version (built for the special series of races held in 1996-7) and the 30-off GTR built in 1999 for another special series and also for endurance racing.

More prosaic is the LMA prototype and a cutaway LM002. Another highlight is the unashamed space given to the Formula 1 project, with an engine on a stand and examples of Lotus 102, Larrousse and Minardi Formula 1 cars. It is probable that only through the exhibits in the museum that most enthusiasts will realise just how deeply Lamborghini has been involved in powerboat racing over the years and how successful the larger-capacity V12 engines have been.

Above all, the museum represents very dedicated professionalism in its approach to display and presentation. Entry is free (although large parties must give advance

warning) and it is open on weekdays from 9.00am to 12.30pm and from 2.30pm to 5.00pm. It is closed at weekends and in August. There is also a shop, selling Lamborghini regalia and the like, run by a volunteer rather than by a member of the factory staff.

The address is Museo Lamborghini, via Modena 12, 40019 Sant'Agata Bolognese. The telephone number is 00 39 051 6817716.

If you are in the area, other museums devoted to high-performance cars are worth a visit. Firstly, Ferrari has a museum at Maranello and although the exhibits are disappointing, a visit is justified. There is no Maserati museum, except for Matteo Panini's extensive private collection on the family Parmesan

Top: On the upper floor of the museum Lamborghini has a Forghieri-designed Formula 1 engine on a stand with (nearest to camera) a Larrousse-Lola and (behind it) a Lotus 102. Above: Part of the main road car section of the airy museum, giving a clear view of the last Countach – a silver 'Anniversary' model – and a stunning Miura SV.

cheese farm near Modena.

Some 100 miles away is the Alfa Romeo collection at Arese, outside Milan, and situated in the company's former headquarters. The factory is all now sub-let apart from the museum and the historical archives. In my experience, you must make advance arrangements to visit the collection, which is profoundly impressive.

Powerboat Racing

The company's involvement in powerboat racing can be traced back to 1968 when Ferruccio Lamborghini installed a 4-litre V12 engine in a powerboat. The Lamborghini company also built their own boat, called the *Quetzal*. It was not a serious undertaking, but the company later realised that the supply of engines for Class 1 offshore racing had good commercial prospects. So Lamborghini set up a small engineering group in the Research and Development department.

The design of the first engine, the L800, closely followed Bizzarrini's original power unit, but it had a displacement of 7,973cc. It was available in two forms, with fuel injection for racing and with carburettors for fast recreational use. Several of the leading racers of the time, among them Count Renato della Valle, agreed to use the Lamborghini engine and in 1984 della Valle won the round-Britain race. From this flowed a

The Spirit of Norway, which won the UIM Class 1 World Offshore Championship three times in six years – seen during its 2003 Championship year.

number of orders.

These successes continued and della Valle won the Italian Championship in 1985 and both the European and Italian Championships in 1986. In the latter year Lamborghini adopted electronic fuel injection in place of mechanical injection and three years later four-valve cylinder heads were introduced.

By 1994 the V12 Lamborghini powerboat-racing engine had a capacity of 8,172cc (there was a capacity limit in this class of racing of 8,200cc) and a power output of more than 900bhp. The company had also developed a four-speed electronic gearbox with automatic gear selection. That year Norberto Ferretti and Luca Ferrari powered their Lamborghini-engined *Giesse Philosophy* to a win in the World Championship. In 1995 Lamborghini-powered boats won four races, but the Champion-ship winner was a boat that used the Lamborghini electronic gearbox with a Sterling engine; the Ferretti team took second place. In the 1996–98 period teams with boats powered by Lamborghini engines won the World Championship each year. The

manufacture and sale of powerboat engines contributed substantially to Lamborghini profits and in 1999 it was decided to set up a new powerboat engine subsidiary, Motori Marini Lamborghini SpA. Between 1984 and 1992 Lamborghini built around 150 racing powerboat engines.

The Championship-winning boat in 1998 was Norwegian Bjørn Rune Gjelsten's *Spirit of Norway*. With vastly experienced Englishman Steve Curtis at the throttle, *Spirit of Norway* won four of the eight Championship races, took six out of eight pole positions and gained the European, World and Pole Position titles. Another European Championship for *Spirit of Norway* followed in 2002.

The 8.2-litre V12 Lamborghini engine that powered the 2002 Championship winner, Spirit of Norway.

Bibliography

Books

Bellu, Serge, *Lamborghini, Tous les Modèles Année par Année*, Editions EPA, 1987

Joliffe, David, with Willard, Tony, *Lamborghini, Forty Years*, Motor Books International, 2004

Lamborghini, *Tonino, Onora Il Padra E La Madre, Storia di Ferruccio Lamborghini*, Éditions Universitaria, 1997

Lyons, Pete, *The Complete Book of Lamborghini*, Consumer Guide (US), 1988

Marchet, Jean François and Coltrin, Peter, *Lamborghini Miura*, Osprey, 1982, reissued by Mercian Manuals, 1999

Pasini, Stefano, *Lamborghini Miura*, Éditions Automobilia, 1988

Pasini, Stefano, *Lamborghini: Catalogue Raisonné*,1963-84, Éditions Automobilia, 1985

Rive de la Box, Rob and Crump, Richard, *Lamborghini Guide, 1963-1973*, Transport Bookman, 1974

Rive de la Box, Rob and Crump, Richard, *History of Lamborghini*, Transport Bookman, Second Edition, 1975

Magazines

Autocar (UK), *Autosport* (UK), *Car* (UK), *Car & Driver* (USA), *Classic & Sports Car* (UK), *Classic Cars* (UK), *EVO* (UK), *Modern Motor* (Australia), *Motor* (UK), *Motor Sport* (UK), *Motor Trend* (USA), *Road & Track* (USA), *Sporting Motorist* (UK), *Sports Car Graphic* (USA), *Top Gear* (UK)

Index